D1577913

Dedication

He was a deputy sheriff, a mayor, a state representative and now a school committee man, but I remember him best as the Master and Keeper of the Lawrence Jail and House of Correction in Massachusetts. Bill Ryan is a master of whatever profession he pursues, and he's a man of many talents. When I was elected High Sheriff of Essex County, he was the first person I hired to assist me. With Ryan being a Republican and me being a Democrat, his appointment caused much consternation among the hierarchy of the Democratic Party. I was, in fact, called before a special council of the party at Haverhill to justify my actions. After listening to this group for some thirty minutes on the reasons why I shouldn't have hired a Republican and why I should have hired a Democrat, I said to them, *"If you have a better man than Ryan to administer this jail, by all means, give me his name now."* There was silence – they knew of no better man for the job.

Because of his enthusiasm, compassion, progressiveness and dedication to duty as administrator of a correctional institute, I dedicate this book on *"Cruel and Unusual Punishments"* to William H. Ryan of Haverhill, Massachusetts and Twin Mountains, New Hampshire. He, more than any man I know, lifted the antiquated Essex County penal system from the Dark Ages into the Twentieth Century.

– Bob Cahill

Copyright, Old Saltbox © 1994   ISBN: 0-9626162-9-X

Cover photo: Hanging scene from the PBS television miniseries, *"Three Sovereigns for Sarah,"* by Nightowl Productions of Martha's Vineyard. Combined photo by Bob Cahill and Mikki Ansin, Cambridge, MA.

Editors: Jean Henry and Keri Cahill
Sketches: Eric Rodenhiser and Ursina Amsler

OLD SALTBOX PUBLISHING
20 Locust Street, #202
Danvers, MA 01923

Almost every New England family owned a slave or indentured servant prior to the Revolutionary War, and the most common discipline then was whipping. Right, is a newspaper ad of 1769, similar to ones appearing in local papers on a weekly basis throughout New England.
Advertisement courtesy of the American Antiquarian Society, Worcester, MA

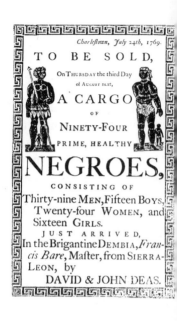

Charleftown, *July 24th,* 1769.

TO BE SOLD,

On THURSDAY the third Day of AUGUST next,

A CARGO

OF

NINETY-FOUR

PRIME, HEALTHY

NEGROES,

CONSISTING OF

Thirty-nine MEN, Fifteen Boys, Twenty-four WOMEN, and Sixteen GIRLS.

JUST ARRIVED,

In the Brigantine DEMBIA, *Francis Bare,* Mafter, from SIERRA-LEON, by

DAVID & JOHN DEAS.

Elizabeth Canning, shown here at an English court in a 200 year old drawing, was sentenced to death for swearing at another woman. Just before her meeting with the hangman in 1754, she was reprieved and offered transport to America as an indentured servant, which she accepted. She was one of thousands sent here from Britain for committing petty crimes.

2

Introduction

When I was Essex County Sheriff and Master and Keeper of the Salem Jail and House of Correction, which was built in 1811, I would sometimes eat lunch with the correctional officers in a little side room off the jail kitchen. One day, I looked up from the lunch table and spied a trap door overhead. *"What's that?"* I asked two of the old-timer guards. They looked at each other with knowing smiles, and one replied, *"That's the hanging trap, where those executed in the last century fell through to their death."* We were munching on sandwiches where some ten to fifteen people had once swung, twitching and gasping for their last breaths. From the moment the function of the overhead trap door was revealed to me, I could never enjoy another meal in that room.

I had run for Sheriff as an opponent to capital punishment. Hanging, gas, lethal injection, firing squad, and the electric chair, just never seemed like humanitarian ways to punish criminals, no matter how terrible their deeds. By murdering a murderer, it seemed to me that we were degrading ourselves to his low level in an attempt to seek justice. Some demented criminals, in fact, wanted death, and we, through capital punishment, were only granting their wish. Life imprisonment without parole, I believe, is the best punishment we could provide for the worst offenders. Maybe in time, the offender will understand the severity of the crime and repent, but with capital punishment, there is no time for real repentance and penance. Certainly, hanging or lethal injection is no deterrent to others who pursue a criminal life, but the possibility of living and working at menial tasks for the rest of one's life behind bars might be.

During the days of Pilgrims and Puritans in New England, there weren't many jails, and the few there were could be escaped from with little effort. The deterrent for crime in those days was mutilation of the body – whipping, branding, cropping of ears, slitting of noses, cutting off of a limb, and of course, burning at the stake and hanging. People were hanged for minor offenses, such as shoplifting and stealing chickens. Little regard was paid to human life. By the mid-1700s, over half the immigrants in New England were indentured and involuntary white servants and black slaves, and a *"master"* could hit or maim such a servant or slave at will. For petty crimes, one would be held up to ridicule in a stock or pillory, where fellow villagers were urged to hurl insults and filth from the streets. Our illustrious patriot and Massachusetts Governor, John Hancock, announced that he believed *"mutilating or lacerating the body is less effective as a punishment than an indignity to human nature."* Many suffered these indignities for breaking a multitude of ridiculous laws introduced by the Puritans, a few of which are in effect to this day, and are known as the *"Blue Laws."*

One such law was passed in 1649, and remained active for almost 50 years. It read, *"Whereas, there is manifest pride openly appearing amongst us in that long hair, like women's hair, is worn by some men, into periwigs, or after the manner of ruffians and barbarous Indians, contrary to God's word. It is a thing uncivil and unmanly, whereby men do demean themselves and do corrupt good manners."* The penalty was a stiff fine, and if the man or boy didn't immediately cut his hair to a respectable length, his neighbors would do it for him at the court house. There was *"no dancing in taverns,"* not even *"at weddings,"* according to a 1631 law, and as late as 1809 at Boston, *"masquerade balls are forbidden because it is detrimental to morals."* For almost a century, Puritan church laws dictated a strict moral code for all New Englanders, and the residue has lasted for over two centuries, dying a slow death. Some of the old laws, however, reappear from time to time in modern society. For example, a 1643 law read that, *"he who smokes in the street is liable to a fine, but a man may smoke if on a journey five miles from any house"* – this one looks like it may be revised soon. Another that perhaps should have been revised read: *"No young man under twenty-one or young woman under eighteen is permitted to be outside after nine o'clock at night without parental permission."* This would certainly help to solve the growing and serious juvenile crime problem in America today. The 1644 law went on to read: *"Young people must not meet in company, unless for religious purposes, on Saturday or Sunday evenings."* Another law for young people, personally written up by Governor John Winthrop of the Bay Colony, read that, *"If any young man attempts to address a young woman without the consent of her parents, he shall be fined five pounds silver for the first offense, ten pounds silver for the second, and imprisonment for the third."* Connecticut did Massachusetts one better, by adding: *"Young men are forbidden to inveigle or draw the affections of any maid, whether it be by speech, writing message, company-keeping, unnecessary familiarity, disorderly night-meetings, sinful dalliance, or gifts, to be punished by whipping and fines."*

Our ancestors and forefathers, it seems, were especially strict about matters of sex and morals. Bachelors could not live alone and had to live with other families, and Winthrop tells us that, *"If any man makes a motion of marriage to any man's daughter, not having first obtained leave and consent of the parents, he shall be punished either by a fine or corporal punishment, or both."* Yet, Governor Bellingham, who served at Mass Bay shortly after Winthrop, married a 22 year old maid without such permission, and Bellingham was over twice her age. Also, being governor, he decided to wed himself, which many others believed was illegal. *"You can't wed yourself,"* he was told by one judge, who insisted he be tried for his offense in court. If that be so, the governor insisted, then he would try his own case, and he would decide the judgment of innocence or guilt. With that comment, the magistrates had the governor forcibly taken from the court and fined him for *"disorderly marriage."* This infuriated Governor Bellingham, but shouldn't have upset him, for the penalty for adultery, which he was guilty of, was death by hanging.

Another of the Puritan elite who had woman problems and didn't seem to practice what he preached, was Judge Samuel Sewall. Sewall was one of the witch-hanging judges of Essex County in 1692, responsible for the deaths of many innocent victims. He also was constantly trying to seduce the Widow Denison, to the point where she threatened to inform the constables if he didn't stop molesting her. Sewall's famous diary, which became public after his death, revealed his inner feelings about Mrs. Denison. *"My bowels yearn towards Mrs. Denison,"* he wrote, *"but I think God directs me in his Providence to desist..."* If he hadn't been a judge, he most certainly would have spent hours in the stocks and pillory for his advances and would have been given 22 stripes of the whip.

For all their strict religious teachings and silly moral laws, it's obvious that rank had its privileges in Puritanical days, and that men were just as bold in pursuing women then as they are now, only then it was against the law. The Pilgrims, and especially the Puritans, however, continued to flog themselves into conformity, often killing those who wavered ever so slightly from their principles. This book is about these people, their laws and their victims, their modes of punishments and the terrible tortures many had to endure in the name of justice.

A master directs his slaves in preparing a new garden.
A live sketch by Anne Marguerite de Marigny, wife of America's French Minister in 1816.

Slave Phillis Wheatley, a noted poet (Boston, who was freed in 1774.
Portrait artist unknown.

Puritan in the stocks, ridiculed and preached to by his neighbors.
From "our Country" by Benson J. Lossing, New York Public Library.

6

The Nantucket Jail, 1805 with stocks and pillory the popular punishment for petty criminals.

I

Sex, Slaves, and Serving Maids

Many today have a misunderstanding of how and by whom America was first settled. To be sure, pious Pilgrims and Puritans were predominant in the first boatloads to the New World in the early 17th century, but they weren't alone. With them came slaves and servants. Landing at Plymouth from the MAYFLOWER in 1620 were 40 Pilgrims, or *"Saints"* as they called themselves, 40 *"strangers,"* and 18 white servants, who were bound by law to wait upon the Saints. On the ship TALBOT that arrived within the year of the MAYFLOWER, there were 35 new settlers for Plymouth, and they were all servants. The same is true of the first Puritan settlers of Boston and Salem, who arrived a few years later. Approximately one-quarter of their company were servants, who could better be described as *"white slaves."*

Most of these people were poor folk between the ages of 18 and 30 – with some younger – who were forced to come to America from the urban squalor of Ireland, Wales, Scotland, and England. Other servants provided for their trip across the ocean to this new land by indenturing themselves to either the captain of the ship, or to a *"master,"* who paid their way, in return for four to seven years of hard labor. Often, the captain auctioned off these servants once he reached an American port, gaining a substantial profit. Some ruthless sea captains hired gangs of thugs to capture young men and women off the port city streets of the British Isles and confined them in vessels until they reached America, where they were sold into servitude. This same procedure was often followed in the late 1600s and early 1700s along the coast of Africa to acquire black slaves to sell for profit in America, where the need for menial laborers was great. If these servants and slaves, black and white, had not been available to New England's first European settlers, these pioneers would never have succeeded in transforming the brutal wilderness into productive farms and thriving villages. As it was in the first year here, for both Pilgrims and Puritans, fifty percent of their population was wiped out by sickness and exposure to the fierce winters. Exactly half of the servants died at Plymouth in 1620-21, among them an eight-year-old boy named More who had been an orphan in England. He had been forced into servitude and transported to America, per order of the Lord Mayor of London. His seven year old brother Richard lived through the first winter and served his master, Mr. Weston, for 14 more years, later moving as a free man to Salem.

Although many young European boys were forced into white slavery, some were shipped off into indentured servitude willingly to New England with the consent of their parents, for the purpose of learning a trade or occupation. The child would sign on with a farmer or a craftsman for as long as 13 years, or until he became 21, and during that time would live with his *"master."* By law, the master had to *"provide sufficient meat, drink, and apparel, lodging and washing,"* but often these were the most meager of provisions, and the master beat the boy for the slightest infraction, or for no reason at all. Yet, poor folks and sometimes even the gentry of New England, introduced their children to this callous system to assure that their offspring could some day earn themselves an adequate living at a respectable trade or occupation. Under most of these service contracts, the boy could be bought or sold to another master, if the first was not satisfied with his work, and he could be rented out at any time for any kind of labor. In early New England, almost all boys and some girls were *"bound out"* at age eight to work for others as servants.

At Puritan Salem in 1639, a shop owner named Perry was placed in jail for constantly whipping his little apprentice boy until he struck the boy so many times that he killed him. Five years later, William Franklin dragged his unruly apprentice boy Nathaniel Sewell to appear before the Boston magistrates, but when he got there, the boy was dead. Franklin was arrested. *"I was only trying to reform the lad,"* he pleaded. *"Can't a man correct his own bound boy?"* The magistrates found him guilty of murder, and he was hanged. Philip Fowler of Boston was brought before the magistrates for abusing his boy-servant Richard Parker a few years later, but Fowler only received a warning to not continuously *"hang the boy up by his heels as butchers hang beasts for slaughter."* At

Newburyport, Mrs. Sarah Emory reported that *"Reverend Samuel Tomb was dismissed as pastor, because of ill-treatment of a little girl, bound as a servant in his family. It was alleged that, being unmercifully whipped for every slight offense, to screen herself, the child became adept at deceit. To punish her for lying, the minister tied her tongue to her great toe."* Young John Grant of Boston reported that his master, Mr. Simmons, *"Tied me to a cradle and pulled off all of my clothes to my shirt and whipped me with three cords tied to a stick that brought blood. Then he asked me if I loved him. I said Yes, and he beat me again. He also beat Betty (an indentured servant maid) so greatly that I fainted."* Plymouth records of 1642 reveal that a 17 year old servant boy named Love Brewster performed a sex crime which Governor Bradford called *"too horrible to mention."* Reverend Chauncy of Duxbury called it *"carnal copulation – an unnatural sin."* Love Brewster confessed and was hanged for the offense.

Servants and slaves in New England were rarely hanged, but they were often whipped or beaten. Many times their only recourse was to run away. Old Colonial newspapers of the early 1700s are filled with advertisements offering rewards for runaway slaves or servants: *"Reward of three pounds offered for return of Margaret Collins, aged above thirty years, remarkably large, fond of company and drink, very impertinent and talkative when in liquor."* Another read: *"Irish servant girl named Catharine Lindon, much pock-marked, a thick chunky girl, with her hair tied and it is almost black; she is supposed to be with child; had on, and took with her, one petticoat, with red, black, and white stripes, one fine shift, one bed sheet, one linen bed gown, one striped, half-worn shoes, and perhaps other clothes that are not yet missed - twenty shillings reward."* And another Irish servant runaway of the early 1700s, Jane Shepard, is described in the press as *"of fair complexion, pretty fat and lusty, about 5 feet 3 inches high, has black hair and is about 23 years of age. She smokes tobacco and her under jaw teeth are black."* One runaway Scotch girl, who owed her master Ralph Sutherland seven years of work after he paid her passage from Scotland to America, was returned after she had traveled only a few miles. Sutherland tied her by the wrists to his horse's tail and made her jog behind as he galloped back to his farm. Exhausted, she stumbled, frightening the horse, which knocked Sutherland out of the saddle, and the horse ran off with the servant girl dragging behind. When the runaway horse was found some miles distant, the girl was dead, her head beaten to a pulp. Although Sutherland was tried and sentenced to hang for his cruel treatment of the girl, influential friends persuaded the magistrates to set him free. Sutherland's punishment was to spend the rest of his life with a hangman's noose around his neck. He lived to be 99 years old, dying in 1801 at home. He was found in bed with the hangman's noose still tied to his neck; he had worn it every day and night for over 57 years.

More times than not, the runaway servant was caught and returned to his or her master, receiving a whipping for the unsuccessful effort. John Powell not only advertised in the paper for citizens to be on the lookout for his runaway servant, but advertised again when the servant was found. He reported that *"he had only gone into the country cider-drinking and will again repair watches and clocks in the best manner and at reasonable rates."* Indentured servants, of course, weren't paid for their labors, but received only room and board and clothing, and thus if they made extra money for their masters, like John Powell's watch repairman, they were all the more valuable to their masters. Often times sea captains would advertise newly arrived shiploads of servants by their trade, rather than their body size, as was usually the case with African slaves. A typical ad, appearing almost on a weekly basis in the Boston Gazette throughout the early 18th century, read: *"Arrived Wednesday, the ship GEORGE, John Adamson, Commander, from Ireland, who has on board several Irish men, women and boys - servants, among whom there is several tradesmen, as carpenters, weavers, tailors, and blacksmiths..."* The cost of shipping one servant to New England from the British Isles might cost a ship owner or captain up to $30.00 in expenses, but the servant could be sold at auction or through the newspapers at a port city for about $100.00, a skilled worker bringing an even greater profit.

In Ireland and Scotland, political prisoners or those convicted of petty and serious crimes could be exiled by the magistrates *"to the Colonies."* In England, pickpockets, debtors, thieves, and felons could ask the judges to banish them to America, and the judges usually complied. Shiploads of convicts arrived in New England in chains from the 1630s until the Revolutionary War, and were sold as indentured servants to carry out their sentences as farmhands, maids and laborers, their *"masters"* unaware of what crimes they committed in the old country. One American who greeted a convict-ship as it docked here, reported *"the horror aboard...a poor man chained to a board in the hole, not much above 16-feet long, and more than fifty of the most dreadful creatures I ever looked on..."* An estimated 25% of all convicts shipped from England to America in the 18th century as servants, died enroute, and an added 35% died before they fulfilled their seven to 14 year obligations as indentured servants in America. Columbia University historian Richard Morris estimates that *"more than 50,000 convicts were transported here from the British Isles prior to 1775,"* some 10,000 of them from one jail alone, London's famous Old Bailey. Most prisoners were forced to serve seven years as servants in America, and murderers were sentenced to serve 14 years. The advantage of convict-servants, who were usually auctioned off at local taverns, was that they were cheaper to purchase than other indentured servants, for *"His Majesty the King,"* paid for their transportation to America. Some truly nasty criminals sold at real bargain prices.

By the mid-1700s Americans were up in arms about becoming the asylum for England's worst felons. Ben Franklin wryly suggested that, *"the Colonies should requite the Mother Country's generous gifts of jail bait by return shipments of rattlesnakes."* In a more serious vain, Ben added that, *"the emptying of their jails into our settlements is an insult, not to be equaled even by emptying their jakes (toilets) on our dinner tables."*

A Boston newspaper reporter wrote, *"It is very surprising that thieves, burglars, pick-pockets, cut-purses, and a horde of the most flogitious banditti upon earth, should be sent as agreeable companions to us! What can be more agreeable to a penurious wretch, driven through necessity to seek a livelihood by the breaking of houses and robbing upon the King's highway, than to be saved from the halter, redeemed from the stench of a gaol, and transported, without expense to himself, into a country, where, being unknown, no man can reproach him for his crimes, where all his expenses will be moderate and low. There is scarce a thief in England that would not rather be transported than hanged...We want people, 'tis true, but not villains."* The British press responded that *"It is only decent to give transgressors another chance under stimulating new conditions."*

Ben Franklin became even more emphatic in his complaints. *"The instances of transported thieves advancing their fortunes in the Colonies,"* he wrote, *"is extremely rare, but the instances of their being advanced to the gallows here, are plenty...Might they not as well been hanged at home?"* Franklin's complaints, and the complaints of other worried Americans, fell on deaf ears – and the convicts kept coming. Not all, of course, were dangerous criminals, and many were exported for petty crimes. Some, merely stealing bread in urban England to feed their starving families, were known to be *"banished to the Colonies."* In the year 1755, of the 2,000 shipped to America in chains, some 400 were women, and 88 were children.

Even from America's beginnings, convicts and con-men came to New England in search of their fortunes. It was where one could become *"rich all of a sudden,"* said Captain Wollaston, who arrived to develop a new colony in 1625, just 22 miles north of Plymouth. With him was the aristocratic lawyer Thomas Morton, with *"thirty servants, and provisions of all sorts."* Within two years at their new settlement, called Mount Wollaston, it was obvious to the Pilgrims at Plymouth that these *"mad men and pettifoggers"* were not going to make it in the wilderness. The Captain was forced to sail to Virginia to sell some of his servants as slaves, *"at a good profit,"* and he called to England by letter for more female indentured servants, preferably criminals that he could buy cheaply. Wollaston finally moved to Virginia for good, but Morton, with a few men and a bevy of female servant girls, remained at what the Pilgrims began calling *"Merry Mount."* It fast became a community of drunken binges and debauchery, and Morton began inviting all his neighbors to his wild parties. Some local Indians came, as did servant girls from Plymouth, and this infuriated the Pilgrims. Some Pilgrim servants girls ran off to Merry Mount and never returned, enticed by Morton's poetic broadbills that he tacked to trees and to his Maypole, which was the site of lewd dancing at The Mount. One such sing-song poem read,

"Drink and be merry, merry, merry boys.
Let all your delights be in Hymen's joys,
Make green garloons, bring bottles out,
And fill sweet Nectar freely about,
Uncover thy head and fear no harm,
For here is good liquor to keep it warm."

Although Morton considered his orgies with servant girls *"harmless mirth by young men who desire no more than to have wives sent over to them from England,"* Myles Standish, the military leader of the Pilgrims, captured him and his men at gun point and shipped them back to England. Another who was banished from Merry Mount was a wealthy Englishman named Christopher Gardner. He was living there with an indentured servant girl that he called his cousin, and he was known to have two wives in England. The Pilgrims and Puritans were well rid of these scoundrels who took advantage of servant girls after enticing them into the wilderness, but history does not reveal what happened to the girls. Were these innocent maidens from the hill-farms of Ireland, Scotland and England, or were they port-city street walkers of the British Isles, convicts, who volunteered to join the wild men of Mount Wollaston?

Women, be they slave, servant, prostitute or housewife, had an extremely difficult time in 17th century New England. Indentured servant girls, at the mercy of their *"masters"* for some seven years, and black slave girls, who remained at their mercy for a lifetime, could be sold at auction to the highest bidder at any time. This situation led to the birth of many illegitimate children, which masters most often refused to support. For bastardy, the penalty was 21 lashes of the whip, but another law in effect at the time was that, *"no gentleman or any man equal to a gentleman shall be punished with whipping unless the crime be very shameful."* Therefore, it was inevitably the maid who was whipped, and not her male partner, which often was her master. She was usually reluctant to accuse her master at any rate, for by doing so, the magistrates would remove her from his home and have her sold elsewhere, often having to leave the child behind to the care of the county. The crime of adultery appears in the General Laws of Massachusetts in 1658, with a

13

punishment of two whippings *"and the persons convicted to wear two capital letters 'A. D.' cut in cloth and sewed on their uppermost garment, on their arm of back; If they remove the letters, they will again be publicly whipped."* Nathaniel Hawthorne revealed this punishment of displaying the letter *"A"* on the outer garment in his novel *"The Scarlet Letter,"* and like his heroine, poor Hester Prynne, history reveals that it was usually the woman alone who was forced to wear this embarrassing symbol and not her male counterpart. Most often accused of this sin were unmarried servant girls. To make it even tougher on these unattached females in the Colonies, Governor Winthrop introduced a law in 1638 making it illegal to marry a servant girl; *"corporal punishment"* being the penalty for any male Puritan who attempted to do so.

If a man servant was identified as the father of a bastard child, he could be charged with adultery and forced to provide extra service to his master to pay for the child's expenses for a period of eight years, or until the child itself became eligible for indentured servitude. More times than not, however, the father was allowed to go free without penalty or charge. There are numerous examples of this in the 17th and 18th centuries: *"Elizabeth Dunwell – whipt for having her third bastard child. Thomas Goodale blamed – not arrested."* Two women charged Jacob Cheesmore of Newbury for two bastard children, *"Cheesmore denies charge and goes free."* In Salem, 1715, *"Hannah Day-bastard child dies, blames Mister Nicholas Webster of Manchester – Constable refuses to arrest him."* In 1724, Mary Mathews murdered her bastard child and is made a slave under the Sheriff for five years, thus avoiding the hangman. The father of the child, John Parron, *"fined three pounds and ten shillings."*

Serving maid pregnancies were often blamed on the quaint New England custom of *"bundling,"* which, according to Webster, means *"to lie in the same bed with one's sweetheart without undressing; a former courtship custom, especially in New England."* It was an ancient custom as well for the Celtics – Scots, Irish, and Welsh, who obviously introduced bundling here through the servant class in the 1600s. In some areas of New England it was still practiced well into the 18th century. Dedham, Massachusetts historian Erastus Worthington writes in 1828 that,

14

"premarital pregnancies were lately occasioned by the custom of females admitting young men to their beds." About the same time, Washington Irving wrote, *"to this sagacious custom, therefore, do I chiefly attribute the unparalleled increase of the Yankee tribe; for it is a certain fact, well authenticated by court records and parish registers, that wherever the practice of bundling prevailed, there was an amazing number of sturdy brats annually born unto the state, without the license of the law, or the benefit of clergy."*

Old Puritans and Pilgrims considered bundling an innocent practice of keeping warm during the cold winter nights. They saw no evil in it, if both maid and suitor kept on layers of clothes, and were well versed in religion and chastity. Sometimes strangers, male and female, slept in the same bed for the sake of warmth and comfort, but over the years, as religious fervor slackened, so too did willpower under the bedclothes and blankets. Birth records reveal that from 1780 to 1790, *"nearly one-third of New England brides were with child before the marriage,"* and this does not take into account the many clandestine co-habitations that produced a bounty of illegitimate offspring. Most unmarried women in early America were poor servants, and those with children were drastically impoverished, which often forced them into lives of crime. From 1670 to 1680, 62 single women, mostly servants, were penalized in Boston for *"fornication and adultery,"* and 51 others for such sex offenses as nude-exposure and prostitution. For adultery, servant girls were sometimes hanged, and for prostitution, the law was also strict and explicit: *"Every baud, whore, or vile person shall be severely whipped at the carts-tail, through the streets, with 30 stripes and then be committed to the House of Corrections, to be kept with hard fare and hard labor."* Before constables whipped these girls at the portable cart, the girls were stripped naked to the waist, which seems a travesty of justice since their crime was often nudity. Now they weren't just exposed for one or two Puritan men to gawk at, but were being viewed naked by the entire village, including the children. An example of this convoluted justice appeared in the Boston Gazette of 1753. It read: *"On King Street, a female accused of lewdness, was exposed nearly naked on a scaffold near the Townhouse, for the space of an hour,*

*facing each of four cardinal points fifteen minutes, suffering the most
disgusting and brutal treatment by a mob."*

English justice, especially coupled with Puritan justice, often didn't
make much sense. One law that was on the books here in the 1660s, as a
carry-over from Queen Elizabeth's dynasty, was that, *"any woman who
entices a man with false hair, Spanish hairpins, or high heeled shoes,,
shall be punished as a witch,"* and these were the days when witches were
burned, boiled, and hanged. It's strange that Queen Elizabeth would pass
such a law, for she was bald and owned over 60 wigs herself. Hannah
Lyman, 16 years old, of Northampton, Massachusetts, flaunted the law by
"wearing wicked apparel," in 1676. Court records reveal that *"she was
wearing silk in a flaunting manner, in an offensive way...also flaunting it
in court."* Hannah was obviously a brave soul, or a foolish one, we'll
never know which, but she paid for her rebellious spirit by being fined.
Surprisingly, she was one of 38 female Puritan servants brought before
the magistrates for similar offenses in Boston in 1676. It seems that by
1676, one hundred years before the great American Rebellion, women,
being led by servant girls, began a revolution of their own here, in an
effort to lift the heavy yoke of oppressive Puritanism from their shoulders.
At Ipswich, Massachusetts in April of 1682, eight girls, two of them
servants, were arrested to stand before the Grand Jury for *"folding their
hair, frizzing and knots, and for wearing silk scarves."* Although it was
considered a serious offense, with a serious penalty of whipping if found
guilty, the girls took the court order lightly, which seemingly befuddled
the magistrates. Two of the girls were taken to court, *"John Roger's
servant and Captain Appleton's maid,"* the only two servants in the group.
They admitted to the jury and judge that they *"folded and frizzed their
hair,"* but they were not punished, because *"none appeared to give
evidence against them, and they were discharged."*

Ten years later in nearby Salem, another group of nine young girls,
four of them servants, boldly began announcing that their neighbors, and
in some instances, their masters, were witches. Two of these girls later
admitted that they *"did it for sport,"* but within a year managed to have 19
citizens hanged, one old man crushed to death as a penalty for standing

mute, and at least two more died of malnutrition and exposure in the Salem jail. The witch hysteria at Salem was stopped by the Governor, but only after the girls had accused his wife of witchcraft. The impoverished, mistreated and persecuted serving maids of Puritan society, with their pre-teenaged friends, managed to usurp the power of their elders to strike fear into the hearts of a New England society that had scorned them since its inception. Black slaves were also deeply involved in the witch hysteria. In fact, Tituba, the Afro-Carib slave of the Puritan minister of Salem village is, to this day, blamed for the practice of voodoo as cause for the hysteria and the ultimate witch hangings. She was imprisoned but was not hanged as a witch. Mary Black, another African slave of Salem village, was accused of witchcraft by servant girl Mercy Lewis, as was Candy, the young slave of Salem's Mrs. Hawkes. Candy went to court and admitted being a witch, showing the magistrates how she made little rag puppets as images of neighbors which she stuck pins into to hurt these hated neighbors. Candy, however, escaped being jailed or hanged by blaming her *"mistress"* Mrs. Hawkes of being a witch and teaching her how to be one. In Salem and surrounding villages, slaves and servants managed to master their betters, and for a brief period cleverly became the accusers rather than the accused.

After a *"good whipping"* by her master, Reverend Samuel Parris, black slave Tituba admitted telling the girls stories of black-magic and sorcery, which seemingly stimulated their persecution of neighbors. When the slave was led into the meeting house with *"heavy chains upon her hands and legs,"* she confessed that, *"I go to witch meetings riding upon a stick."* Tituba practiced witchcraft. It was part of her religion of voodooism, which is still practiced in Barbados, the island that Tituba lived on before she was taken to Salem as a cook by Reverend Parris. Being a sorceress gave Tituba power, not only among her own people, but among the superstitious Puritans. Throughout New England there were black *"witch-doctors"* that blacks and whites came to for advice and for herbal cures for a variety of sicknesses and injuries. *"Old Ham"* was a black male witch of the Isles of Shoals and Strawberry Bank, New Hampshire, in the 1650s. *"Tuggie Bannock"* was a noted black witch of the 17th century in Narragansett, Rhode Island. She was the daughter of an African king, and slave to Rowland Robinson, and both blacks and whites acknowledged that she had great powers. If anyone got her angry, she would make *"evil puppets"* of their likeness out of dough and leave it on their doorstep as a curse, which would literally send them into fits. She also made effigy puppets of wood, which she burned, causing great pain to her human victims. Villagers were so impressed and so frightened of her powers, that they paid her way back to Africa to visit her family. For a time, slave Tuggie Bannock was the most powerful person in Narragansett, as was Chloe Spear, soothsayer of Boston. Their contemporary was *"Black Phillis"* of Barrington, Rhode Island, via Africa, who was considered the most skilled herbal doctor in New England. There were many other black slave fortune tellers and herbal doctors, who supposedly practiced the black arts, but by displaying their skills and charms, flirted with the hangman. John Indian, Tituba's slave-servant husband, once his common wife was imprisoned, began embroiling himself in the witch trials by accusing others, until his master gave him a thrashing, and he wasn't heard from again. *"Wonn,"* a black slave belonging to John Ingersol, helped to get Bridget Bishop hanged at Salem, testifying that she *"bewitched the horses so that they run down da swamp on they bellies,"* and that she turned into a black cat and pinched him as he sat at dinner. The black female slave of Peter Tuft of Charlestown, Massachusetts blamed Elizabeth Paine and Elizabeth Fisdick of witchcraft in 1692, as revenge for past cruel treatment to her by the two women. *"Peter,"* a black slave of Newport merchant Jon Powell, *"took fits and convulsions and was in great agony,"* when he visited Salem courthouse in 1692. He cried to the great congregation of Puritans who had gathered there that he was *"bewitched,"* but, *"Mister Powell applied his horse-whip to Peter, with such effect that he gladly returned to his duties."*

The Puritans feared pompous and progressive slaves and servants. Chloe Spear, a slave woman who kept a journal, wrote that, *"Under penalty of being suspended by two thumbs and severely whipped; my master said it made Negroes saucy to know how to read."* At about the time of the Salem witch trials, a New London, Connecticut Puritan reported, *"I went to the Courthouse to hear the Examination of sundry witnesses concerning the cruel whipping of Zeno, a slave of Mr. Nicholas Letchmer. There was a great concourse of people and the court chamber would not hold all."* Were these people angry with Mr. Letchmer for beating his slave almost to death, one wonders, or were they all just curious to see what penalty the slave master would get from the court? Letchmer received only a warning not to be so *"heavy-handed."* Nathaniel Keen of Kittery, Maine was taken to court in 1695 for beating his slave woman to death. The magistrates found him guilty only of *"cruelty,"* and Keen walked away a free man. At Salem, prior to the witch trials, a servant, *"for malicious and scandalous speeches,"* was *"whipped, had both ears cut off, was fined a heavy sum and was banished"* from all Puritan Colonies within New England, which means that the Pilgrims wouldn't take him in either. Where would this poor earless servant go? Roger Williams, an outspoken minister who was also banned from Salem and all other Mass Bay communities in 1631, went to live with the Indians in what is now Providence. There he founded Rhode Island and America's Baptist religion. All outcasts – slaves, servants, runaways, witches, Catholics, Baptists, Quakers, Jews, criminals, and whomever, were welcomed at Roger Williams' Rhode Island, which literally became a thorn in the side of Puritanical Massachusetts and Connecticut.

If a slave was caught stealing in Massachusetts or Connecticut, according to a 1646 law, his or her punishment could be death; *"and against the heinous and crying sin of man-stealing,"* also, death, the latter seemingly a law passed against Rhode Islanders who enticed unhappy slaves and servants to settle in their province. In Puritan New England, punishment seemed to depend on who the thief was and who the victim. At Essex County in 1640, for example, a Puritan in good standing, one Mister Plaistowe, and his servant boy, were caught stealing corn from the local Indians. Their punishment was: *"Plaistowe will no longer be called Mister, and his servant to be whipped 22 lashes."* Servants and former servants who were caught stealing were not only whipped but also had their servitude lengthened: *"Israel Gould, for stealing sheep, whipped 135 stripes and sold into hard labor for damages and costs."* Some thieves who were citizens and not servants were also sold into servitude for their crimes: *"Thomas Brown stole 42 pounds worth of clothes from George*

Stacey. He is to pay triple damages of 126 pounds, and if he can not pay, is to serve Stacey in servitude for ten years." These were tough penalties indeed, but only to be experienced by the poor and lower class of the new world, whereas gentlemen of wealth and prestige could literally get away with murder. It was New Hampshire settlers who saw the cruel system for what it was and passed a law in 1718 which read: *"No longer shall inhumane severaties by Evil Masters or Overseers be used toward their Christian Servants...And any murder of a Slave is to be a Capital Offense..."* Although New England Quakers did have servants, they were opposed to slavery from its inception, and in 1730, Quaker Eli Coleman of Nantucket wrote: *"I am against the despicable practice of making slaves of men."* To have such a statement published in an newspaper when almost every New England family held one or two black Africans as servants or slaves was tantamount to sacrilege.

Prior to the Revolution, Sarah Emery informs us, *"At that time nearly every family owned one or more Negro slaves."* Most New Englanders today are not aware that slavery was rampant here prior to the birth of abolitionism. Estimates are that there were some 1,000 black slaves here in 1690, and within 50 years, there were 1,500 black slaves in Boston alone. In Newport, Rhode Island, slave capital of New England, 20% of the population was black in 1755, and 40% of the population of Charlestown, Rhode Island was African born, or first generation African-American. But by this time, some blacks had earned or had been given their freedom from slavery. All New England ports were home to slave traders by the year 1700, and Newport claimed 120 vessels active in the slave trade as early as 1690, each delivering about 200 or more Negroes in chains from West Africa to the West Indies each year, where most were sold for molasses to make rum in Newport. *"Rhode Island is founded by rum and slaves,"* was an old saying, and the clergy justified the capturing and selling of human beings by shouting from their pulpits, *"We save black souls."* The justification was that Christianity was not being taught in Africa, and as one Newport minister preached: *"We thank you God that Providence has brought to this land of freedom another cargo of beknighted heathen to enjoy the blessings of the Gospel."* Most of these black knights that came into New England were children, for most masters wanted to personally

20

train young slaves in proper house keeping or farming chores. They sold on the auction block for sixpence per pound in the 17th century. Few Yankee masters wanted more than two slaves, and those purchased would usually spend their lives working side by side each day with their masters, but one slave owner, Abraham Redwood of Newport, owned 238 slaves in the mid-1700s. The Reverend Cotton Mather of Boston, leader of the Puritan society in the late 1600s, when criticized by Quakers for owning slaves, said: *"These Negroes are of our own household, more clearly related to us than many others are."* Yet, when Negroes and their masters began naming newborn black babies *"Cotton Mather,"* he became enraged and accused them of *"blasphemy."*

"Likely Negroes, both male and female, from 10 years to age 20, imported last week from Africa" – typical ads like this one that appeared in the <u>Hartford Courant</u> in 1766, brought the average farmer and householder to the slave market every Saturday, or at least once a month. Slaves that knew English, rather than slaves *"directly from Africa,"* were preferred. New Englanders liked slaves that had *"seasoned"* for a year or two in Barbados or Jamaica. learning English jargon and British discipline before being shipped north. Since Africans were not accustomed to, nor did they like, the cold wintry months, it was often a threat and a penalty for unruly blacks in the West Indies to be *"carried North."* Therefore, many who came here were *"refuse,"* and the *"worst sort,"* as Massachusetts Governor Joseph Dudley called them in 1708. *"They are slaves who could not be sold elsewhere,"* he complained to the slave merchants, *"and they make the worst of servants."* Governor Samuel Cranston of Rhode Island said of New England slaves, *"they are of turbulent and unruly tempers and most are imprudent."* Five slaves of William Pepperell of Kittery, Maine died in 1719 after only a few days of experiencing winter weather, which prompted slave merchants to place ads like this one in the <u>Boston Gazette</u>: *"Gambia slaves are much more robust and tractable than any other slaves from the coast of Guinea, and are more capable of undergoing the severity of the winter seasons in the North-American Colonies."* But no matter where these slaves came from, Africa or West Indies, robust or not, about 30% of them died on their way to, or shortly after they arrived in

New England, many from cold and disease, but some from the club and the whip.

At Salem in 1733, a black slave woman *"cut open her stomach with a knife to commit suicide,"* saying as she did so that she was *"returning to her homeland of Africa."* Chloe Spear, the Boston black fortune teller explained her actions as *"a rebirth."* Chloe said that the Salem slave believed that *"just like a young moon comes after the old moon goes away, the first child born into the family after an older one dies, be the same person come back again."* Slavery was such an agony to some that they felt their only escape was suicide. Coupled with the belief that when one died he returned to Africa and the family he left behind, death seemed sweeter than life. There were many examples of this *"suicidal martyrdom,"* as it was called. Old Gin Cole, a slave of Deerfield, Massachusetts in 1715 at old age, gathered all the trinkets she had saved over the years – string, bits of glass, pottery – into the death bed with her. Her last words were that she was bringing them home to Guinea with her to show her father. Phillis Wheatley, an educated slave who was bought at the Boston market in 1759 at age seven, was writing poetry in perfect English as a teenager. She expressed her deep sorrow and longing for Africa in one of her poems:

> .....*"I, young in life, by seeming fate*
> *Was snatched from Afric's fancy'd happy seat:*
> *What pangs excruciating must molest,*
> *What sorrows labour in my parents' breast?*
> *Steel'd was that soul and by no misery mov'd*
> *That from a father seiz'd his babe belov'd:*
> *Such, such my case, And can I then but pray*
> *Others may never feel tyrannic sway?"*

Phillis Wheatley was considered one of the luckier slaves, for not only was she educated, but when her mistress died in 1774, she was freed. She married a former slave who was a dandy. He provided her with three children and then left her to cope on her own, forcing her to become a servant. She died at age 31, two of her children dying before her and the third, shortly thereafter.

Although monogamy was the law here among blacks and whites, polygamy was common among slaves, as was premarital and extramarital sex. As Reverend John Sharpe of Connecticut wrote in 1713, *"Negro marriages are performed by mutual consent, without the blessings of the church."* June Larcom, a slave of Beverly, Massachusetts in the mid-1700s had four children by slave Jethro Thistle, but they weren't married, and all this under the watchful eyes of Puritan preachers, who would not allow such behavior within their white flocks. Mulatto children of black and white parents became quite predominant in 18th century New England, and no one could explain this phenomenon better than Frederick Douglas, the abolitionist and most famous fugitive slave of the 19th century, when he said, *"Thousands are ushered into this world annually, who, like myself, owe their existence to white fathers, and those fathers most frequently their own masters."* Even pious Puritan Samuel Sewall, one of the witch-hanging judges of 1692, wrote in his Journal that, *"It is too well known what temptations masters are under, to connive at the fornication of their slaves."*

Abortion of slave children was not unusual in colonial New England. Most masters didn't want the expense of raising a black child, especially in his own household if the child was his, and the mistress of the house was unaware of his extra-curricular activities. Abortion then was not a crime until the fetus began to move in the womb, and there were many books available on various methods of aborting a fetus, as there were herbal purgatives, such as juniper and snakeroot. Those who were not aborted were born into a lifetime of slavery, more often than not taken from their mothers shortly after birth and given to others to raise. They were passed around to neighbors and friends like newborn puppies or kittens, sometimes sold, and often swapped for a sack of potatoes or some other commodity. The callousness of masters concerning slave children is reflected in this advertisement which appeared in the <u>Boston Evening Post Newsletter</u> on July 10th, 1761: *"Exchange or Swap – African children for*

Negro men who are strong and hearty, tho' not of the best moral character."

"*Grandfather Smith had a black maid and great-grand sir Little, a man slave, and they were married,*" wrote Newbury's 18th century historian Sarah Emery. "*If there were children, the owners would divide them. Two were born, but they were swept away with those of their masters, by the throat distemper, the year it made such ravage in New England.*" Ms. Emery also writes that, "*Most of the families in Byfield in the Olden Times held one or more slaves, and there was usually quite a sprinkling of the sable hue amongst the pupils of the district school.*" Byfield, Massachusetts, it seems, was an unusually liberal village, for most New England communities either had a separate school for the black children, or gave them no education at all, prior to the Revolution. White children were whipped and given the switch quite often during their school days as a penalty for the slightest infraction of school rules and regulations, and although few records are available, we can assume that black children had it even tougher at school. Sarah Emery, in her book, "*Reminiscences of a Nonagenarian,*" published in the mid-1800s, supplies us with an example of a "*Negro boy who the master of the school always slapped on the head.*" His white classmates, angry that their black colleague was forever singled out for abuse, "*saturated his woolly hair with oil and put him up to a prank, which he was sure to get a slap for. The heavy-handed master,*" who Ms. Emery describes as a "*great dandy, always foppishly attired*" (in other words, he was a nerd always wearing fancy clothes), "*coming up the aisle and noticing the delinquent, he gave him a sound cuff of the side of the head, which splattered the oil all over his fine clothes.*" Sarah ends her story there and doesn't tell us what terrible penalty the boy had to pay for soiling the school master's clothes and supplying a good laugh for his schoolmates.

The whip used on the Negro slave was not the schoolmaster's switch, cut from the branch of a tree, although that hurt quite sufficiently. "*It was six or seven feet in length, made of cowhide, with a plated wire on the end of it,*" as former slave William Brown described the "*Negro Whip.*" Used more in the South than in New England, and sold in every local variety

24

store and hardware store there, it was well known here, especially in Newport. Wealthy plantation owners of Virginia and South Carolina sailed North each year in the mid-1700s to spend the summer months in Newport. The first Newport mansion was built by Virginian slave merchant Godfrey Malbone, who, like the other Southerners, came North to escape the summer heat. He was a strong disciplinarian with his many slaves, and held them responsible for all his material possessions. If a dish was broken by accident, the slave responsible for dishes would have to pay with extra work. A young lieutenant in the British Army, visiting his fellow Virginian at Newport in 1756, dropped and broke an expensive punchbowl. Godfrey Malbone informed the lieutenant that he would have to pay the slave responsible, otherwise the slave would have to pay, possibly with his hide. The young lieutenant made out a cash check right on the spot and handed it to the nervous slave. The check read, *"By cash, to Mr. Malbone's servant, four pounds, signed Lt. George Washington."* George would return to New England some twenty years later as General Washington to break something else – the stronghold of England's tyranny on black and white Americans alike. It was truly the Revolutionary War that made white New Englanders more sensitive to the injustice of slavery, as they battled for their own independence, and every New England state abolished slavery shortly after the war. Most blacks, however, found it even more difficult to be free than to be a slave. An editorial in the Hartford Courant in 1774 said it all in one sentence: *"Nothing is more common than for men to treat Negroes and to speak to them in the most contemptuous manner, as tho' they did not belong to the same species."*

A French visitor, Alexis de Tocqueville, 57 years later, made the following observation: *"In New England, free blacks are deprived of their rights in the midst of a population that is far superior to them in wealth and knowledge, where they are exposed to the tyranny of the laws and the intolerance of people."* In the big cities he noted the free blacks *"perform the meanest effaces and lead a wretched precarious existence."* One wonders if his observation would be much different today.

Old laws for slaves remained in effect even after blacks gained their freedom. These were ridiculous laws, such as, *"No Negro or Mulatto may leave his master's house upon the breaking out of a fire in the night time; nor shall he be found in the street near the scene of a fire, upon pain of being arrested and sent to the common gaol, and afterward whipt at the House of Correction."* This was a 1723 law which remained on the books throughout the 18th century in Massachusetts. *"No Negro or Mulatto shall be on Boston Common after Sunset,"* was another, and whipping remained the penalty of a white co-habiting with a Negro, throughout the 1700s and into the 19th century, well after slavery was outlawed. A Boston ordinance, passed by the city fathers in 1769, remained in effect throughout the century, but was not enforced after the British troops left town. It read that *"All Negroes found outside after dark without a lantern shall be arrested."* A freed slave, *"Old Tony,"* was discovered by the town's night watchman *"prowling about in total darkness,"* and he was arrested. At his trial he pleaded not guilty, and surprisingly was acquitted. He had witnesses that saw him carrying a lantern. *"Tis so,"* said Old Tony, *"I carried a lantern, but it jest weren't lit."* The law was immediately changed to read *"No Negro shall be outside after dark without a lit lantern."*

There are thousands of examples of injustices to freed slaves in New England, as there are to Afro-Americans to this day. Other nationalities, races, and religions suffered greatly here in New England as well, during our Puritanical growing years, but few suffered the degrading depravity of Africans and Afro-Americans. Our own deeply prejudiced society and cruel legislation is not that long forgotten, and not that fully eliminated. Although we don't like to admit it, white New Englanders still sometimes offer Afro-Americans a subtle yet very real version of cruel and unusual punishments.

26

In the 18th century, after a criminal was hanged, his body was often saturated with tar and hung in chains at a busy crossroads or on an island for mariners to view. This was expected to be a deterrent for others who might be contemplating a life of crime. The corpse would usually mummify and remain on display for many years. It was called "gibbeting," and a slave named Black Mark, gibbeted on the Cambridge Road in 1755, was mentioned by Paul Revere in the report of his Midnight Ride in 1775.

The wooden horse, or "stang," was a popular punishing device in the military through the Civil War. Although the horse remained stationary, an unruly soldier was made to ride it for hours with fifty pound weights tied to each foot. The pointed edge of the horse's back would cause great pain.

Poor Captain Asa Kimbal of Salem, after arriving in port after a long voyage, "publicly kissed his wife on the Lord's Day at noon." when she went down to the docks to greet him. He was made to remain locked in the pillory for the rest of the day as a punishment.

At Portsmouth, New Hampshire in the late 1600s, this cage device was their means of punishing criminals. It is described as being "twelve feet square, barred on four sides, with stocks within it and a pillory on the top."

28

II

The Black and Blue Laws

The Pilgrims' Governor Bradford blamed the 1642 crime-wave in America on *"undesirable immigrants,"* Puritan Governor Bellingham in Boston wrote to him that, of their priorities, the increase in crime was number one – *"The first is concerning heinous offenses in point of uncleanness."* The new country was only twenty-two years old and was already going to hell. *"Some kind of wickedness did grow and break forth here,"* Bradford told Bellingham, the two being the leaders of the New England Colonies. He marveled that such a thing could happen in *"a land where the same was so witnessed against, and so narrowly looked unto and severely punished...And yet all this could not suppress ye breaking out of sundry notorious sins...and that so many wicked persons and profane people should so quickly come over into this land, and mix themselves amongst us...."*

Many foreign visitors to this New World blamed the Pilgrims and Puritans themselves for unscrupulous criminal acts. *"The inhabitants seem very religious, showing many outward and visible signs of an inward and Spiritual Grace,"* wrote England's Edward Ward in 1699, *"But tho they wear in their faces the innocence of doves, you will find them in their dealings, as subtle as serpents. Interest is their faith, money their God, and large possessions the only Heaven they covet....Many of the leading Puritans may, without injustice, be thus characterized."* He concluded that our founding fathers were, *"Saints without religion, traders without honesty, Christians without charity, magistrates without mercy, subjects without loyalty, neighbors without amity, faithless friends, implacable enemies, and rich men without money."* Wow! What a put down. Imagine how the Pilgrims and Puritans must have felt when they read Ward's report, and this coming only some fifty years after these pious Americans had gathered in Connecticut to determine for themselves who they really were. In 1640 they decided and voted that, *"The Earth is the Lord's, and the fullness thereof; Voted, that the Earth is given to the Saints; Voted, that we are the Saints."*

Based on this, we can certainly conclude that they were proud, and probably conceited, believing that they were better people than all other human beings who lived in the world around them. Even in the beginning, America's first settlers of Pilgrims and Puritans were considered religious fanatics by the European neighbors they left behind. They came here to escape religious persecution and cruel English laws that not only restricted them but imposed punishments for expounding their beliefs. Once settled here, they did not wish to follow English law. The principals set forth in the Holy Bible would be the laws of the new land, which they preached, and for awhile, practiced. The philosophy of our founding fathers was the exact opposite of America's philosophy today. John Cotton, Cotton Mather's grandfather, Puritan minister and civic leader, constantly exclaimed from the pulpit that no distinction should exist between church and state – *"All is derived directly from man's spiritual comprehension."* America was ruled by the church and regulated by church discipline.

At Charlestown, Massachusetts, on August 23, 1690, aboard the ship ARABELLA, Governor Winthrop appointed himself, with Deputy Governor Dudley, Governor Endicott of Salem and three others, as magistrates of the new Bay Colony. They would have *"power in all things that justices of peace hath in England for reformation of abuses and punishing of offenders, and may imprison any offender, but not inflict corporal punishment without the presence and consent of some one of the Assistants."* This not only gave these six men complete discretion on what was a crime and what wasn't, but what an offender's punishment might be, including death, as long as some assistant, who the governor hired, agreed with the verdict. Within five years, the Puritan Freemen of the Bay Colony demanded that the governor provide the growing communities with written laws. A committee of Puritan ministers and magistrates was appointed in 1635 by the governor to make a list of laws, but the laws weren't ready until October of 1641. In December of that year, the Great and General Court of Massachusetts adopted the laws, 100 of them, and provided the basics of what became the American court system, including the Supreme Court, Court of Appeals, and County Courts. Still basically ruled by the clergy, many of the resultant laws were as restrictive as they were ridiculous, and the court punishments were torturous, and often as bloody and bruising as any English torture invention of the Dark Ages.

A whipping post or cart, stocks and pillories stood near the courthouse or meeting house of every New England village and town, always readily available for the infliction of suffering and pain. Jails, called *"gaols,"* were built in the larger towns, but sometimes there was only a cage, usually built on the village green where culprits were kept for all to see and ridicule. The cage built at Portsmouth, New Hampshire in the late 1600s was a fancy device: *"Twelve-feet square, barred on four sides, with stocks within it and a pillory on the top."* The stocks and pillory, locking in head and hands and sometimes feet as well, were not as painful as they were embarrassing for the one who had to endure them. More often than not, rotten eggs and other filth were thrown at a person locked up in a pillory, and sometimes, as part of his or her punishment, an ear, or both, would be cut off, or the prisoner would be branded with a hot poker on the cheek or forehead. Branding and maiming were the penalty for many offenses, including: theft, vagrancy, counterfeiting, forgery, slander, manslaughter, and religious improprieties. In retrospect, it seems that those who criticized church and state received the cruelest of punishments. Phillip Ratcliffe, for example, the first to attempt to develop a fishing industry at Marblehead, Massachusetts in 1631, made some *"foul and slanderous invectives"* against the government, and the magistrates decided that *"he shall be whipped, have his ears cut off, be fined 40 pounds, and banished out of the limits of this jurisdiction."* Governor Winthrop, in his mercy, delayed the banishment of Ratcliffe, *"as it was winter and the man must have perished,"* but Deputy Dudley, a man of tougher mold, who later became governor of the Bay Colony, complained that Winthrop was being too lenient.

In the *"Body of Liberties Laws,"* adopted in 1641, blasphemy was a capital offense, with a penalty of forty lashes of the whip and a fine for the first infraction, and banishment or death for the second. As many women were banished into the wilderness as men for the sin and crime of blasphemy, and if lucky, were taken in and cared for by one of the surrounding Indian tribes. For *"exorbitancy of the tongue in railing and*

31

scolding," usually a female crime, the offender was *"gagged or set in a dunking-stool and dipped over head and ears three times in some convenient place of fresh or salt water."* John Dunton, a Londoner visiting New England in 1686, wrote home in disgust, revealing that, *"For the crime of cursing and swearing, they bore through the tongue with a hot iron. For scolding others, they gag and set them at their own doors for certain hours, for all comers and goers to gaze at..."* At New Hampshire's Isles of Shoals, one Joan Ford, fishwife, was brutally whipped in December of 1665 *"for calling the constable a horn-headed rogue and a cow-headed rogue."* Her wounds not yet healed, she confronted the constable again, *"reviling and abusing him with very evil speeches."* Joan Ford was whipped again, thirty lashes on her bare back, and she was banished from the islands, but when the constable returned to the mainland, she sailed back to the Isles. Fisherfolk were different than the day-to-day Puritans and Pilgrims. They were, by far, a rougher lot, and it was usually the leader of a fishing crew who was the authority in fishing villages and island communities, not the constable or sheriff. Cotton Mather concluded that fishermen and their women were so lawless because *"Satan has induced them to become slaves to the bottle."*

Many times the fishermen of New England took the law into their own hands, and their punishments could be even more cruel than the official Puritan and Pilgrim penalties. One favorite treatment for those they thought deserving was tar and feathering, a popular punishment for tax collectors and informers just prior to the Revolutionary War. The most famous victim of tar and feathering was Floyd Ireson of Marblehead. He and his crew aboard the schooner BETSY had refused to come to the aid of another commander and crew of Marblehead fishermen in the midst of a storm off Cape Cod. The ACTIVE, the schooner of the distressed crew, finally sank, but the commander and crew survived and returned home to tell the townsfolk of Skipper Ireson's inhumanity. The men and women of Marblehead, all fisherfolk, marched to Ireson's home, dragged him from his hearth into the street, stripped him of his clothes, cooked up a tub of hot tar, and with brushes and brooms, painted his body with it. Then, before the tar dried, they pelted him with torn bags of goose feathers, which stuck to his skin. He was then seated in a dory and dragged through the streets of the town, accompanied by an ever increasing mob, who jeered and spit at him as they rolled along. When the bottom fell out of the dory, he was transferred to a cart and ridden through the winding streets as neighbors and old friends whipped his bare back with switches and whips. After some three hours of mob rule, he was escorted home, more dead than alive, but Ireson survived. He later blamed his misdeed of leaving the schooner in distress on his cowardly crew. "Skipper Ireson's Ride," was later made famous in a poem by John Greenleaf Whittier, and Ireson himself was lost in a wintry sea shortly after his experience of being tarred and feathered. Many believed he committed suicide.

Fishermen, seamen, and merchant mariners living along New England's seacoast made up a large percentage of the country's population, and in their constant dealings with foreign ports, provided a continuous flow of new citizens. "By this means," complained Governor Bradford of Plymouth, "the countrie became pestered with many unworthy persons." These were anything but Saints, and many of them scoffed at religion, especially the religion espoused by the Pilgrims and Puritans. Court records of the 1600s are filled with complaints against men of the seaside villages and towns, cursing the prevalent religions, their preachers and teachers. "George Harding of Marblehead, fisherman, to pay a fine or be whipped for saying that he intended to be a member of the Puritan congregation next year, and would then have his dog christened." In 1644 at Salem, "John and Stephen Talbie, for unbecoming speeches about a dog in the water, but not proving the baptizing of him," they were admonished and fined court costs. "Joseph Fowler, Gloucester, to sit in stocks one hour and a half or to pay fine, for saying there are seven or eight liars in the church, and if one would lie soundly, he be fit for the church." Nicholas Bickford, Isles of Shoals, 1684, "for profane swearing and multilying of oaths; fifteen lashes and to pay twenty-shilling fine, or an equal payment in fish."

If women swore or used profane language, they often had their tongues perforated with a hot iron, or were whipped, whereas the penalty for men cursing usually was less severe, sometimes only a fine of a few shillings. Much depended on who was being cursed, for what reason, and how many times they were cursed. Part of the law read that: *"He who swore more oaths than one at a time, before removed out of a room, building, or company where he so swore, should be fined only twenty shillings."* However, if one should curse to *"Injure any particular person,"* he should be *"fined, confined in stocks, and severely whipped, as the facts warrant."* For example, Goodwoman Gregory of Springfield, Massachusetts, was heavily fined and made to sit in the stocks in 1640, *"for using many oaths,"* and saying to her neighbor, *"Before God, I could break thy head."* Whereas one John Lee, *"for calling Mister Ludlowe a false-hearted knave,"* was merely fined. Unfortunately, John Lee appeared before the Mass Bay magistrates again six months after his first offense, *"for speaking reproachfully to Governor Winthrop, saying he was but a lawyer's clerk and a just-ass."* Since the Governor in those days was all powerful, representing not only the executive but the legislative and judicial branches of government, John Lee found himself in deep trouble. Winthrop, as we established earlier, was a humane man, and Lee was only fined and whipped. Lee later got in trouble again for *"abusing a maid of the Governor's, pretending love in the way of marriage."* Across the Charles River at Cambridge, then called New Towne, there was another like John Lee, a critic of the government, named John Allen. He was getting himself into a peck of trouble, cursing and blaspheming. Besides calling the governor some unflattering names, he shouted drunkenly that, *"This country is ruled by redheaded curs and redheaded dogs and redheaded rogues,"* – the governor of Massachusetts, then, as now, was a redhead. Allen was due for a whipping, a fine, and a day in the pillory, unless he repented and asked forgiveness. *"I do acknowledge I have done exceedingly wicked things and abused the honored gentleman...but I hope this honored court will be pleased to extend charity to me,"* pleaded a sober John Allen. *"I never more will by the help of God do any more so wickedly. So humbly submitting myself to the good will of God and your Honor's mercy..."* and he went on groveling for ten minutes, which managed to reduce his punishment to just a fine – his glib tongue getting him into trouble, as well as getting him out. The Praye brothers of Ipswich were another outspoken foul-mouthed pair: *"Richard Praye, fined ten shillings for swearing; ten shillings for cursing; twenty shillings for beating his wife; fifty shillings for contempt of court. Quinton Praye fined fifty shillings for five oaths; fined twenty shillings for two lies."* Another Ipswich *"scold,"* as outspoken women were called in those days, was Elizabeth Perkins. She was taken to court in 1681 for *"opprobrious and scandalous words of a high nature, spoken against a Mr. Corbit and a Mr. and Mrs. Perkins,"* the later being her in-laws. The magistrate called Elizabeth a *"wicked-tongued woman,"* and ordered that she be *"severely whipped on the naked body and to stand at next lecture day in an open place in the public meeting house for all to see, with a paper pinned to her head, written in capital letters the words 'FOR REPROACHING MINISTERS, PARENTS AND RELATIONS' and to pay a fine of three pounds."* Another woman from Taunton, sentenced in 1656 for *"blasphemy,"* was to be whipped *"22 stripes at Plymouth and Taunton on market day, and forever have a Roman 'B' cut out of red cloth and sewed to her upper garment on her right arm in sight."* For a similar crime in Newbury four years earlier, Doctor William Snelling, a *"merry man"* who drank too much, yet cursed often and *"blasphemed,"* received a fine of 20 shillings and a warning from the magistrate. There was obviously blatant sex discrimination by our founding fathers, and a great dislike by them of women who opened their mouths, especially if harsh words came out. The anti-blasphemy law, by the way, was never removed from our ledger of laws, and was last invoked by Joan Chivarini of Framingham, Massachusetts to block the screening of the movie, *"The Last Temptation of Christ,"* in Massachusetts in the year 1988. The law is 300 years old.

"The special sin of women is pride and haughtiness, and that is because they are generally more ignorant and worthless," shouted the Reverend Jonathan Edwards from his pulpit at Plymouth, preaching to our Pilgrim Fathers. English common law allowed *"the infliction of chastisement on a wife by her husband,"* which the Pilgrims and Puritans adopted, meaning that a woman could be beaten by a man using *"a reasonable instrument."* Near the turn of the 18th century, New England women began asking what that *"reasonable instrument"* was. Magistrate Buller of Charlestown responded by stating that *"I hold that a stick no bigger than my thumb, comes clearly within the description of a reasonable instrument that a husband may use to strike his wife."* It

wasn't too long after Judge Buller's statement that the women of Mass Bay Colony banded together and forced a new law to be adopted: *"That every married woman shall be free from bodily correction or stripes by her husband, unless it be in his own defense upon her assault. If there be any just cause for correction, complaint shall be made to authority assembled in some court, from which only she shall receive it."* This was truly the beginning of women's liberation in New England, especially when only a few years earlier in 1658, a woman who committed adultery in Puritan colonies was put to death.

Exactly 100 years later on August 16 at the Cambridge Superior Court, the Boston News Letter reports: *"One Hannah Dudley of Lincoln was convicted of repeatedly committing adultery and fornications with her own Mother's husband, an old man of 76 years of age. She was sentenced to be set up on the Gallows for the space of one hour, with a rope about her neck, and in the way from thence to the Common Gaol that she be severely whipped 30 stripes, and that she forever wear a Capital A to her clothes, and sewed upon her upper garment on the outside of her arm in open view."* Committing adultery and fornication still remains a crime in Massachusetts, and this law was vigorously enforced, usually bringing a jail sentence to guilty parties well into the 1950s.

Ladies of the Night are, of course, committing adultery and fornication on a regular basis, as are their constantly rotating companions, but even in Puritanical Massachusetts, whore houses flourished. One of the first houses of ill-repute mentioned in the 17th century records, is the Widow Thomas' House and Merchandise Shop of Boston, active from 1664 to 1672, until Widow Alice Thomas was taken before the magistrates as a *"common baud."* She was found guilty on five counts: *"1) Selling wine and strong water without a license; 2) Entertaining children; 3) Selling liquor on the Sabbath; 4) Frequent secret and unreasonable entertainment in her house; 5) Lewd, lascivious and notorious persons of both sexes committing carnal wickedness in her house."* She had to pay threefold restitution, but for what exactly is not specified, and she paid a 50 pound fine, plus court fees, which was a very heavy fine for those days, probably close to $5,000 by today's standards. She then had to sit upon the gallows for an hour with the hangman's noose about her neck. She was then stripped to the waist and whipped 39 lashes, more than enough to kill a man. Then she was jailed for a few months and banished. She disappeared into the wilderness for a year, then returned to Boston, promising to pay for the building of a needed seawall if the magistrates would allow her back in town. They agreed, and she returned to rebuild her old business.

The world's oldest profession really got a foothold in Boston in the 1800s. Even today's prestigious Beacon Hill was described in the press in 1816 as a place that *"consists principally of drunkards, harlots, spendthrifts, and outcasts from the country."* Possibly the reporter was writing about the state legislature, which meets on Beacon Hill, but the hill was also known as a notorious haven for prostitutes in the 18th and early 19th centuries. Also in Boston's North End, there was a bevy of activity at a building called *"The Beehive,"* a most popular house of prostitution. The *"queen bee"* was Madame Cooper. She had two pretty daughters and ten female boarders. Men were constantly popping in and out of the hive, a two-story house with many bedroom windows, and this made the neighbors at first curious, and then angry. On the evening of July 22, 1825, as on the evening of Skipper Ireson's ride and the night of the Boston Massacre, an angry mob marched down the narrow unlit streets to the Beehive. There were an estimated 200 men and women carrying axes, pitchforks, tin horns and loud drums. Their faces were blackened and they wore costumes, much like minstrels. They broke down the door and smashed the windows, invading the house, making sounds that one witness described *"would wake the dead."* All furniture and people in the house were thrown out the doors and windows. *"Feathers from all the feather beds, covered the street like a snow storm,"* said one eye witness, and the invaders burned buckets of tar to paint some of the whores and male clients as they tried to escape up the street. Fat Madame Cooper screamed at the top of her lungs as she saw her bordello literally get ripped apart before her eyes. Soon, the rags and feathers caught fire and all went up in flames. *"I tell you sir,"* said the Boston watchman on duty that night, *"It was the scene of a lifetime. The swarm left the hive and few were stung"*

– yet, it was a typically rowdy New England riot, performed for the good of the people, whether they liked it or not.

Women weren't the only second class citizens in early New England. Children, be they rich or poor and of any religion, were often treated worse than farm animals. Among the first Puritan laws and punishments, known today as the *"Blue Laws,"* were a few designed specifically for children. One was that *"the striking of your mother or father is a capital offense, punishable by death, with Judicial discretion."* The Connecticut Puritans added that, *"Any child over sixteen years of incorrigible stubborn and rebellious nature, is to be put to death."* The old adage of *"Spare the rod and spoil the child,"* came to us from England, via the Pilgrims and Puritans. The birch rod or ruler, used to whack the hand or rump of a misbehaving or inattentive schoolboy by his teacher, prevailed into the mid-20th century. A Connecticut boy named Perkins was given an adult whipping in 1890. After going to court, he was found guilty of *"idle behavior at the meeting-house; such as smiling and enticing others to the same evil, and for pulling Benoni Simkin's hair during services, and for throwing another girl on the ice on the Sabbath Day."* In Boston, the law read that, *"Children who behave disobediently and disorderly toward their parents and governors, to the disturbance of families and discouragement of such parents and governors, shall be whipped, exceeding ten stripes."* More than one child died as a result of experiencing the Boston whipping block, and although there is no recorded death of a child after being whipped at school, many cruel schoolmasters relished the power of *"tanning the hide"* of children. One noted Boston disciplinarian was a teacher name Lovell, who whipped boys unmercifully as he made them ride piggy-back, one mounting the back of another, to get his whipping. Henry Brooks, writing from Boston in the mid 1700s, writes, *"the beating of scholars is a practice very common in schools here, for such offenses as whispering and looking off the book. I know a master whose delight, apparently, was pounding and beating little boys. He did not touch the large ones, and yet, he was considered a first rate teacher."*

"There was an aftermath of sorrow," wrote Reverend Eliphalet Nott of Connecticut in the early 1700s, *"when our stern grandfather whipped*

us when we were children after we got home, for being whipped at school." Reverend Cotton Mather of Boston, complained in 1713 that children should be whipped more severely. *"There are knots of riotous young men in the Town,"* he wrote, *"who, on purpose to insult Piety, will come under my window in the middle of the night and sing profane and filthy songs...Tis high time to call in the help of the government for punishing and suppressing of these disorders."* From his pulpit, Mather challenged others to *"Walk among the children in the time and place of their play, and observe the wicked language heard among them, and employ the best methods to nip the impiety of their language in the bud."* Bad language or cursing often resulted in a whack on the head by a ruler-wielding teacher, but a more popular punishment in Puritan New England for a little foul-mouthed pupil was a whipping to the bottoms of his bare feet, while two other schoolmates held him down. Sometimes boys couldn't walk for a day or two after enduring this punishment.

At Hartford, Connecticut, magistrate Richard Malbon had his teenaged daughter stripped to the waist outside the meeting house and whipped until her back looked like raw meat. Her heinous crime was that she had become a *"Friend,"* a Quaker, whom the Puritans and Pilgrims of the early 1600s came to hate more than Catholics and heathens. Quakers came into America, like most others, poor and destitute from England and Ireland. By the mid 1700s, many of them became successful and wealthy traders, merchants, and smugglers, but their treatment in the 17th century was harsh to say the least. Ann Hutchinson of Salem became the first Quaker criminal to be banished from all Puritan and Pilgrim colonies. She preached, as all Quakers did, a doctrine of personal grace, *"devoid of either liturgical rules or ministerial authority."* In other words, the Quakers began spreading the word in New England in 1634, that to be holy and saved, one didn't need a church or a minister, which to the Puritans, was sacrilege. Most Quakers were flogged, many from village to town, and most of the victims were young girls, hardly out of their teens. Many became martyrs as they were hanged on Boston Common. Some fled to Rhode Island and Sandwich and Falmouth on Cape Cod, where they found asylum and freedom to speak and worship as they pleased. Those who remained behind in the Mass Bay Colonies or Plymouth suffered terribly: *"Mary Fischer and Ann Austin, Quakers, stripped to the waist, bound and dragged and flogged. The knot upon ye end of the whip of the Minister, striking ye nipple of one, did cause it to burst open, to her great discomfort and paine, and causing great delight to those round about."*

It was a crime in the early 1600s to house a Quaker, or even invite one into your house. One identifiable mark of a Quaker was that they never took off their hats, even inside a building, and they said *"thee and thou"* a lot. At York, Maine in 1635, Thomas Taylor had to sit in the stocks for a day, his crime being that, *"He be too familiar to Captain Raynes and he said 'thee and thou' too often."* The King of England finally interfered and demanded that Americans stop treating Quakers so badly. The Puritans complied, but within a few years, they were torturing and hanging others, mostly older women, also innocent victims, whom were called *"witches."*

Whipping seemed to be the most popular form of punishment for three centuries here in New England. There were even *"scourgings,"* as they called whippings, on Sabbath days, when people weren't allowed to do anything else but sit, listen to sermons, and pray. Even the military, Army and Navy, adopted *"flogging"* as their prime punishment. Kennebunk, Maine, 1655 – *"Punishment is given on training days,"* a young militia lieutenant informs us. *"The culprit is taken to the training field at the head of a military company to have twenty-five stripes on his naked back and to have his neck and heels tied together for a full hour."* Regulation punishment in the Navy, for any minor offense, up to 1776, was twelve lashes. Sam Romilly tells us that the *"flogging of three Navy men in 1806, was inflicted with such horrible severity that they all died in less than 24 hours."*

"The cat usually had a rope handle two-feet long – one end whipped and nine pieces of line spliced into it, with two-foot tails, with Turk's Head knots on the ends, spliced to each tail." This was the infamous *"Cat-O-Nine tails"* used for discipline in the military, adopted from the English. *"It was delivered with a man's full strength,"* says 18th century sailor Dudley Pope, *"and it was clear that a man standing braced but unsupported*

would have been knocked down by one blow...One lash would break the skin and severe bruising would result." Thirteen year old Army Private Gamaliec Bradford, Tenth Massachusetts Regiment, 1776, from Duxbury, witnessed a friend of his desert the Army, get captured, and stand before the whipping post to receive 100 lashes – a punishment that would surely kill him. *"I felt for the poor fool,"* writes Bradford, *"and went to the Commandant to intercede for a remission of the stripes...To my request, he agreed to dispense with half the stripes."* Bradford's foolish friend, however, couldn't endure the agony of fifty stripes, and he died shortly after the punishment was completed.

In the early 19th century, *"a stout, slovenly dressed woman,"* from Rhode Island named Caroline Arnold Williams, took the U.S. Navy to task. She began a campaign of essays, articles and lectures on *"the brutish punishment, as dangerous as it was degrading, called flogging."* She prodded the Congress to outlaw it, and whenever she met up with a naval officer, she confronted him on the subject. With the help of Massachusetts novelist Richard Dana and his best-selling book, *"Two Years Before the Mast,"* Congress and the U.S. Navy finally relented, and in 1850, there was no more flogging in the military. Whipping as a punishment was also stopped in the New England states in the 19th century, but less than fifty years ago, John Barbieri was found guilty of beating a woman, and was given six months in jail plus *"twenty lashes of the whip."* This was is Delaware, where whipping remained a punishment until 1972. In that year, Judge Stewart Lynch sentenced a thief named Tal Basler to be whipped, pay $500 in fines and be sentenced to 25 years in jail. Basler appealed and his sentence was reduced to ten lashes of the whip, but was never carried out.

Back in 1876, while visiting the garret of the Newport State House, noted historian Samuel Adams Drake saw, *"a section of the old pillory that formerly stood in a vacant space before the building. Many think the restoration of stocks, whipping-post and pillory,"* concludes Drake, *"would do more today to suppress petty crimes than months of imprisonment."* He would probably find even more advocates today, some 125 years later. Drake goes on to comment that, *"The pillory, which a few living persons remember, was usually on a movable platform, which the Sheriff could turn at his pleasure, making the culprit front the different points of the compass."* Unlike the whipping post, the pillory was used more for embarrassing a guilty person in front of his neighbors and peers, rather than inflicting pain. Sometimes, however, his ears were pinned to the pillory, his nose was slit, his ears were cropped as he stood or sat in it, or he was branded with a letter, which was painful enough, making him easily recognized wherever he traveled as a 'B' burglar, 'C' counterfeiter, 'F' forger, or 'T' thief . Most were branded on the cheek or forehead, and sometimes the hand – the right hand for the first offense, and the left hand for the second.

Essex Gazette, April 23, 1771, *"William Carlisle was convicted of passing counterfeit dollars, and sentenced to stand one hour in the Pillory on Little Rest Hill, next Friday, to have both Ears cropped, to be branded on both cheeks with the letter R, to pay a fine of one hundred dollars and cost of prosecution, and to stand committed till the Sentence is performed."* Charlestown, April 3, 1660, *"One Thomas Browning, burglar, branded in forehead with letter 'B'."* Salem, 1801, *"Hawkins, for Forgery, stood for one hour in the pillory and had his ears cropped."* Walpole, 1762, *"Jeremiah Dexter for passing two counterfeit bills – in pillory for one hour."* Worcester, 1769, *"Lindsay stood on pillory for one hour, after which he received 30 stripes at the public whipping post and branded in the hand 'F,' his crime being forgery."* In that same year at Worcester, a man who sold guns to the Indians stood in the pillory and was branded with a hot poker 'I' on the forehead. When John Bastwick was held in the pillory for calling the ministers unflattering names and had his ears cropped off, *"his daughter stood on a stool, kissed him on the cheek, and placed his ears in a clean handkerchief and carried them away with her."* The last to be locked into the pillory at Boston was John Nichols on April 26, 1805, convicted of counterfeiting. All New England states gave up this Puritanical relic by 1840, but Delaware held on until 1905.

There were other even more hideous torture devices introduced in pre-colonial New England, but none were as popular as stocks, pillory, and whipping post, which all villages and towns were required to have by law. The *"stang"* was used sparingly by Puritans, but was a periodic instrument of pain and ridicule for military men from the French and Indian War through the American Civil War. The wooden stang stood about four feet high, with a pointed back, which the man being punished was forced to sit on or *"ride,"* with fifty pound weights tied to each foot. This *"wooden horse,"* as it was also called, remained stationary, but was quite painful to sit on, especially after many hours. It was invented by the Scots, and therefore, very popular in southern Maine, where the English deposited many Scots political and wartime prisoners in the 17th and early 18th centuries. Kittery, Maine, 1670: *"A militia man road a wooden horse, for dangerous and churtonous caridge of his commander and mallplying oaths."* The Repentance Stool, or *"cutty-stool,"* another Scots invention, was also popular in early New England. It was a high stool, sometimes only one or two-legged, on which a victim would have to sit balanced for a period of many hours. It was usually used in churches and schools to hold delinquents up to ridicule or to publicly rebuke members of a congregation for some sin or evil deed. The disobedient or inattentive schoolboy, forced to sit in the classroom corner on a stool, wearing a *"dunce"* cap, is a 20th century remnant of the *"cutty-stool."*

In 17th century New England, the repentance stool was in constant use at Puritan meeting houses, most frequently for sins of the Sabbath. The Blue Laws of keeping the Sabbath a day of prayer and inactivity were especially strict: *"No man shall run on the Sabbath, or walk in his garden, except reverently, to and from meeting. No one shall travel, cook victuals, make beds, sweep house, cut hair or shave on the Sabbath day. Any person who shall be found smoking tobacco on the Lord's Day, going or coming from meeting, within two miles of the meeting-house, shall pay twelve pence for every such default, to the Colony's use."* Vermont added that, *"No one shall visit from house to house on Sunday, except from motives of humanity or charity, nor shall anyone travel between midnight of Saturday and midnight of Sunday, or attend any ball or dance during that period."* The Pilgrim Sabbath laws were just as strict as the Puritan's, and in 1691, when King William combined the Bay Colonies and Plymouth Plantation together under a new charter, their strange and sometimes silly laws, were also joined. A Plymouth law read: *"No one is to walk down to the water-side on the Lord's Day, nor even the hottest days of summer...And if two or three people, who meet one another in the street by accident, stand talking together, if they do not disperse immediately upon the first notice, they are liable to fine and imprisonment...All journeying on the Sabbath Day is forbidden, except where the traveler is forced to lodge in the woods the night before, but he is permitted to travel not further than the next inn. Transgressors of this statute shall incur a fine of 20 shillings for the first offense, and three pounds for the second. Those unable to pay spend five days in jail or four hours in cage or stocks."* Another Plymouth law, passed by the legislature of Pilgrims in 1658, was that *"Any person who behaves themselves profanely by being without doors of the meeting-house on the Lord's Day, in time of exercises, and there, misdemeaning themselves by jestings, sleepings, or the like, are to be admonished, and if they do not refrain, are to be set in the stocks, and then go before the court."* Gustavus Myers of Plymouth tells us that four years later, the General Court *"forbid Inn Keepers to sell liquor between church services, except to the faint and sick, and that after, it was reported that many complained of ailments, necessitating liquid treatment."*

Many people were arrested throughout the 17th century and well into the 18th for breaking Sabbath laws, for sleeping at meeting, walking or riding a horse, swimming, sailing, quarreling, holding hands, and a variety of other activities. At New Haven, Connecticut, Jonathan and Susan Smith were *"tried in court and fined five shillings and cost, for profanation of the Sabbath, when during Divine Service, they did smile."* John Lewis and Sarah Chapman of New London, Connecticut, were prosecuted and fined in 1670 for *"sitting together on the Lord's Day under an apple tree in Goodman Chapman's orchard."* Roger Scott of Lynn, Massachusetts, *"fined for sailing out of Ipswich River on the Sabbath."* Reading, Massachusetts even had a law concerning dogs on the Sabbath. The 1662 law read as follows: *"Every dog that comes to meeting on the Sabbath, except it be that the owner pays for a dog-whipper, the owner of those dogs shall pay sixpence for every time they come to meeting that doth not pay the dog-whipper."* In other words, no stray dogs were allowed in church, only member dogs whose owners paid the whipper.

As foolish as many of the Blue Laws sound today, they were obviously taken very seriously by our forefathers. Even when church leaders and state officials became more lenient toward Sabbath laws in the mid 1700s, some officials and ministers held onto tradition tightly. In Connecticut in 1751, magistrates made it clear to all *"sheriffs, constables, jurymen, and tithingmen, to watch for and arrest all offenders of the Sabbath statutes, without need of warrants, or they temselves become liable for neglect of duty."* An editor of the Massachusetts Centennial complained in the April 30, 1786 issue, *"To see people riding on Sunday in pursuit of their worldly affairs is so disgusting to the man of true principle, that the neglect of our executive authority of so flagrant a crime is to be lamented."* The Blue Laws concerning the Sabbath, died hard in New England. In fact, in watered-down form, they are still with us, with constant disputes between business owners and police departments about store openings on Sundays. Up until June of 1985, Connecticut had maintained an absolute protection of the Sabbath law, which allowed workers the right not to work on the Sabbath, *"no matter what burden this imposed on employers or fellow workers."* But, the U.S. Supreme Court struck down the Connecticut Sabbath law, upholding the Constitutional principle of dividing church and state. Periodic twitterings of the old restrictive laws do occasionally appear in public to whet our Puritanical appetites, but for the most part, the ancient Blue Laws are dead, and good riddance. In retrospect, however, one can't fail to wonder, did they just die out of natural causes, or were the first Pilgrim and Puritan governors right, when Bradford suggested that, *"Some kind of wickedness did grow and break forth here"*?

*Bathsheeba Spooner, pregnant with child, wife of a patriot and daughter of a
Colonial General, is brought to the gallows at Worcester, Massachusetts on
July 2, 1778 to hang, after witnessing her three fellows in crime be executed.
Thousands came to witness the spectacle but a terrible thunderstorm dampened
their spirits. "She died poorly," said the hangman.*

III

From the Highest Tree

There was probably not a more horrible, exciting, jovial and wretched event in the olden days than a hanging. In New England's pre-colonial days, it was a holiday. Adults were excused from their daily labors and children were let out of school. It was a combination of a carnival, religious ceremony and brutish orgy of boozing and brawling. *"Here is all hurry and confusion, racket and noise, praying and oaths, swearing and singing psalms,"* reported one man after witnessing his first public hanging in 1698. He was further amazed when he studied the thousands who had come to witness the execution: *"Their faces, every one, spoke a kind of mirth, as if the spectacle they had beheld had afforded pleasure instead of pain."* Another eyewitness described a hanging as a *"spectacle so awful, yet so interesting."* The word gallows itself comes from the word *"gala,"* meaning an event or party.

Pie-men and other food and drink purveyors often set up tents or make-shift shops at the hanging scene. The victim was sometimes allowed to stop at local pubs under guard as he was transported from the jail to the gallows, until the victim, hangman, and the spectators arrived on the scene, all drunk. Ministers often complained in writing and from the pulpit that *"hanging days"* were nothing more than *"drunken holidays."* A clergyman always accompanied the condemned to the gallows and usually stood beside him praying as the rope was fitted to his neck, but many times, it was the clergyman and not the one being hanged who became the subject of ridicule from the mob. From the moment a criminal received the verdict *"death by hanging"* from the magistrate, the local minister was at his side, buzzing in his ear to repent his sins so that he might enter heaven and not hell after death. On the Sunday before execution, he was brought to church to be preached at before the entire congregation. Unless he repented, the minister was at his side every minute preaching and praying, adding to his pre-hanging tortures on execution day. Repentive preachings of a chaplain that saved a condemned sinner's soul, or the final words of the condemned themselves (printed up in advance) were often sold at the hangings for a penny apiece. A condemned person who did repent and begged for *"Benefit of Clergy,"* could be reprieved by the minister, and saved from death, sometimes at the last minute. Cotton Mather enjoyed waiting until the noose was around a person's neck before reprieving him or her. During the great harvest of pirates at the Boston gallows in the 1700s, Reverend Cotton Mather was famous for saving one repented pirate out of every crew. The reprieved one was then forced to join the army, or work at hard labor in prison for the rest of his life. *"Benefit of Clergy"* was abolished in 1827.

Sometimes, a frenzied mob or those inclined to think that the condemned person was innocent of the crime, would try to free him; at other times, as the condemned man or woman was hanging, friends and relatives would pull at his or her legs to help death come quicker. This is where we get the old saying, *"He's pulling your leg,"* meaning that someone's telling you a tall tale or is trying to fool you. More times than not, the victim remained alive up to an hour after being hanged, the body dangling at the end of the rope, limbs twitching and throat gurgling. As the victim wriggled in pain, male spectators would shout, whistle and curse, women would screech and scream and children would cry in terror or shriek with laughter. Witnessing a hanging at Boston in 1704, Judge Samuel Sewall writes: *"When the scaffold was let to sink, there was such a screech from the women present, that my wife heard it sitting in our orchard, and was much surprised, for our house is a full mile from the hanging place."* Finally still, with eyes bulging, his body turned blue, and pants filled with his own filth, the victim was dead. Some people in the crowd would rush to the corpse to touch it, believing that doing so would cure them of any ailment or skin disease they might be suffering. Everyone wanted a piece of the hanging rope, for another New England superstition was that the rope used to hang a person brought luck to anyone who possessed a piece of it.

Part of the entertainment at the end of the hanging celebration was watching the relatives and barber-surgeons fight over the body. *"The contests between these were fierce and bloody and frightful to look at,"* wrote an eyewitness. The barber-surgeons needed bodies for teaching students the methods of dissection, and relatives wanted to give the victim a decent burial. *"No man hanged for murder shall be buried until after dissection by surgeons,"* was a 1752 law. All those condemned for rape or witchcraft were not allowed to be buried in consecrated ground and, therefore, were kept out of local graveyards. Doctors feared cutting up the corpses of witches, so those mostly elderly female bodies were dumped in pits near the hanging trees and covered with sprinklings of dirt, in hopes that they would quickly rot and their bones would be carried away by wild animals. Of the estimated forty or more witches and Quakers hanged in 17th century New England, all were innocent of crimes, and of the hundreds of others hanged for various offenses here, it was later determined that almost half were innocent – yet all this grizzly public gore was officially performed, supposedly as a deterrent for the adults and children who witnessed it. It, in fact, seemed to have the opposite effect.

During a last-minute stay of execution of a hanging in Pembroke, New Hampshire in 1834, a disappointed crowd turned on the local sheriff and his men, creating a riot, during which the hangman himself was nearly executed. When John Bonsfield stood at the gallows in 1856 for murder, he fainted when the noose was put around his neck. The hangman and constables sat him in a chair over the trapdoor. He was unconscious when the trap door fell and he dropped with the noose tight around his neck. Bonsfield regained consciousness and grabbed the rope. He then managed to swing his legs back onto the gallows platform. The hangman kicked his feet away, but Bonsfield grabbed the edge of the trapdoor and hung on. The constables and hangman now grappled with him, all to the delight of the crowd, who were cheering Bonsfield on. When they managed to loosen his grip on the trapdoor, he'd swing his feet onto the platform again. This battle of life and death continued for many minutes, the crowd roaring their approval, until Bonsfield inevitably lost the struggle, the two constables hanging onto his legs as he gasped unsuccessfully for air. The crowd then began pelting the hangman and constables with rocks and they had to be escorted to their homes by the militia. At a Boston hanging in April of 1738, it was reported that the hangman was so drunk, that instead of placing the noose around the condemned man's neck, he placed it over the minister's head, and was about to hang him when the local sheriff stepped in to halt the proceedings, which drove the crowd into a near frenzy – they wanted to see the minister hang.

By the mid-1800s, most public executions had ceased in New England. They became private affairs inside the various jails and prisons of New England, the sheriff or under-sheriff being the hangman. However, throughout most of the 1600s, 1700s, and early 1800s, public hangings, with an official hooded hangman, were common occurrences, especially in the large towns. It was one of America's many goulish bad habits brought to New England from mother England. One 16th century English traveler named Thomas Wright, wrote: *"Every town...has a gallows or tree with a man hanging upon it, and it is so frequent an object in the country, that it seems to be considered as almost a natural object of the landscape."* In England, as in New England, people were hanged for minor offenses such as petty theft, pick-pocketing, forgery, and *"shoplifting of anything over five shillings."* In the 17th century, if a person could read the 51st psalm of the Bible without a flaw, he was released, but in those days most people were illiterate. Many professional thieves hired teachers to help them memorize the verse, just in case they were caught and condemned to death. Witches, of course, were hanged, as were gypsies, or anyone of a religious calling that differed from Puritans and Pilgrims. Anyone visiting a suspected witch, or calling on a gypsy for advice, could also receive the death penalty. If those accused and convicted of witchcraft could say the Lord's Prayer without making a mistake, they could be freed from the hangman's noose. George Burroughs, a minister from Maine condemned to hang at Gallows Hill in Salem, Massachusetts in 1692, did say the prayer correctly, with all in attendance to hear, as he stood on the hangman's ladder with the noose around his neck. The Reverend Cotton Mather, sitting on a white horse under the hanging tree, heard him too. Many in the crowd thought Burroughs should be released, but Mather, convinced that Burroughs was the devil incarnate, considered it an evil trick, and demanded he be hanged, which he was. One also would be hanged for *"attempted"* murder, rape, arson, treason, piracy and all the major crimes. George Manley thought that even for his crime of murder, hanging was a cruel and unusual punishment. Allowed to address

50

the crowd from the gallows platform before he was hanged, as most condemned persons were allowed to do, he said:

"My friends, you are assembled to see what? A man leap into the abyss of death! You say that no man, without virtue, can be courageous! You see what I am, I am a little fellow...My Redeemer knows that murder was far from my heart, and what I did was through rage and passion, being provoked by the deceased. Marlborough killed his thousands, and Alexander the Great, his millions, and many others have done the like, and are famous in history as great men. I am a little murderer who ran a debt with the ale-wife, and I must be hanged."

As far as we know, the first public hanging in New England took place at Plymouth in 1630. John Billington, a Mayflower passenger was a *"Stranger,"* not a *"Saint,"* and a *"knave,"* wrote Governor Bradford in his journal, *"and so would live and die as one."* Billington was a complaining troublemaker from the beginning in 1620, and after ten years of harassing and haranguing the Pilgrims, he cornered his hated neighbor John Newcomin in the woods and shot him. The Pilgrims easily found Billington guilty of murder, but they were timid about inflicting the death penalty, and so, *"We took counsel of our friends just come into Mass Bay, and were advised to purge the land of blood."* The Puritans, pleased that the Pilgrims would confer with them on such an important matter, were quick to recommend the death penalty. After all, they would hang someone just for stealing a loaf of bread, theirs being an *"eye for an eye, tooth for a tooth"* philosophy. Governor Bradford requested all Pilgrims to attend John Billington's hanging.

Thomas Morton, another *"knave"* in Governor Bradford's estimation, refuted in his book, New England Canaan, that Billington was the first to be publicly executed in New England. Morton spoke of *"the weaver who was hanged for the crime the cobbler committed,"* at what is now Weymouth, Massachusetts. At Wessagusset , there were Anglicans, the remnants of Morton's Merry Mount, who were reduced to slaves by the local Indians. One was caught stealing corn from the Indians, a crime punishable by death, and the Indians insisted on a public hanging by the whiteman, which they would attend. The thief, a cobbler, was strong and needed in the struggling community, but there was an old weaver in the little community who was dying, and so they dressed the weaver in the cobbler's clothes to fool the Indians. And in a great ceremony at Weymouth, the old weaver was hanged to the satisfaction of the Indians. This was Morton's story, but supposedly, in reality, no substitution was made, and the real thief was hanged for stealing a few ears of corn. There was also a little known hanging at the Wessagusset trading post as early as 1623, when Myles Standish and eight other Pilgrims, before a crowd of invited Indians, hanged a 15 year old Indian boy from a tree because he and his friends were planning to attack the trading post.

At Boston in 1638, the Puritans hanged Dorothy Talbe for the *"unnatural and untimely death of her daughter, Difficult Talbe"* whom she admitted killing, *"to save it from being miserable."* The crime of killing a child was called *"infanticide,"* and it occurred again in 1646, when a young girl named Mary Martin of Casco Bay, Maine, supposedly killed a child in her care. At Boston, she was put through the *"ordeal of touch,"* an old silly but lawful superstition, where one accused of murder is brought before the corpse to touch it, and if it bleeds, the person is guilty, and if the body of the victim doesn't bleed when touched by the accused, he or she is found not guilty. The Puritans believed that God in this circumstance would intercede and inform them who was guilty and who was not. She was made to touch the child, which didn't bleed, *"but blood did come fresh to its face when Miss Martin touched its cheek."* That was enough for the Puritans and she was hanged. The *"ordeal or touch,"* was used quite often in New England to solve murders, and the year before Miss Martin was hanged, another Maine woman, Goody Cornish of Agamenticus, was accused of murdering her husband and dropping his body into the nearby river. The body washed ashore downstream and Mrs. Cornish was brought before her husband's corpse by the local sheriff to touch it. Records reveal that, *"the body did bleed when she touched it."* She confessed and was hanged.

Mass Bay Governor Winthrop informs us in his journal that in 1641, *"Thomas Owen and Sara Hales went to the gallows with their heads covered and a noose around their necks."* They thought they were going to be hanged, apparently for some indecent act, which Winthrop was too embarrassed to mention, but instead they were forced to stand over the trapdoor of the gallows for two hours, then Sara was banished and made to wander in the wilderness. Hanging, in fact, may have been a less cruel fate, unless she made her way to Rhode Island, or to a friendly Indian village. We are not told what Thomas Owen's fate was, but he wasn't hanged. Two years later, however, James Britten and Mary Latham, for seemingly the same offense as Thomas and Sara, also had to stand at the gallows, but they were hanged. Winthrop said that, *"James was a man ill-affected both to our church discipline and our civil government." "Mary Latham,"* writes Winthrop, *"age eighteen, is a proper young woman, who was rejected by one man and married an ancient fellow."* James and Mary first denied that they committed adultery, but then confessed. Mary said that twelve other Puritans had slept with her, some of them quite prominent in the church hierarchy. They, brought before the governor, denied it and went free, but they were made to watch Mary hang.

Young Mary Dyer's crime was that she returned to Boston after being previously banished from all Puritan communities. On October 27, 1659, with Marmaduke Stevenson and William Robinson, she was marched to Boston Common from Boston Jail, under guard of 100 uniformed soldiers. Three nooses dangled from the branches of an old sturdy tree, with a ladder propped under the branches for the victims to stand upon while the nooses were fitted over their heads. The black-hooded hangman would then push each off the ladder to a strangulating death. Governor Endicott forced Mary to wait, with the noose about her neck, to watch her two fellow Quakers hang before it was her turn. After being pronounced dead by the hangman, the two were cut down, Robinson's skull breaking open in the fall. Their bodies were stripped naked by the soldiers and they were thrown into a watery pit on the Common. As the hangman turned to Mary Dyer, many in the crowd pleaded with Endicott to reprieve her. Mary's son was there, and he promised the governor that if he would free her, he would immediately escort his mother to Rhode Island, where they accepted Quakers. Endicott, not wanting to endure the wrath of the crowd, reluctantly agreed, and Mary's son was good to his word, but it took almost an hour to get Mary off the ladder, for she wouldn't come down. *"Not until you annul your wicked ways,"* she told the governor. The soldiers finally had to force her down. Seven months later, Mary was back in Boston, delivering anti-Puritan speeches in the streets and on the Common. It was back to the Common, with a noose around her neck again, she quickly found herself, with over 1,000 spectators there to watch her swing. The governor didn't even give her a chance to make a speech this time, and she was pushed off the ladder without delay. There was such a crowd returning to Salem from Boston that evening, all having traveled the 12 miles to witness the hanging, that the bridge spanning the North River in to Salem collapsed under their weight, severely injuring some 60 people. Since Salem was where Stevenson, Robinson and Mary Dyer were earlier captured attending a secret Quaker meeting at Witch Hill, Salemites had a special interest in the hangings. The North Bridge tragedy, however, made several wonder if God might be displaying His displeasure at the hanging of these three souls who did nothing more than preach the love of God.

The law against Quakers in New England in 1659 was strict and unwavering: *"All Quakers or 'Friends' shall be driven into the wilderness, exiled on pain of death."* Puritan and Pilgrim leaders actually sent out spies to various villages and towns to find and arrest Quakers, whip them, banish them, and/or hang them. One Quaker, William Ledra, was easy to find, for he purposely walked into Plymouth and refused to leave, driving plantation officials to near insanity with his persistent preachings. After a few weeks in jail, the governor offered to release him if he'd pay a small fine and leave Plymouth. Ledra refused. The governor then offered him free passage to England. He refused that, too. The Pilgrims then contacted Governor Endicott at Salem and asked him what to do with the defiant William Ledra. Ledra had, in fact, been at Salem prior to visiting Plymouth, and Endicott knew exactly what to do with him. He had Ledra shipped to Boston under guard, and brought to the big tree on Boston Common. Endicott had his drummers beat their drums so loudly that Ledra's final inspiring words could not be heard by the masses that had gathered, and he quickly joined his fellow Quaker martyrs, his body then deposited in the pit. It wasn't until King Charles II took the throne in

England, that two Salem Quakers, Samuel Shattuck and Edward Burroughs, managed to obtain an audience with him and persuaded him to stop the torture and hanging of Quakers in Massachusetts and Connecticut. King Charles obliged them, and his order to *"cease and desist"* was personally delivered to Governor Endicott by Quaker Shattuck in November of 1661. Endicott was forced to obey, but persecution of Quakers continued well into the 18th century. It was about that same time that Puritans began in earnest to hang those suspected of witchcraft. It was as if the Puritans had to have scapegoats, and needed hangings to vent their anger and frustration.

There were four women hanged in Connecticut in 1647 for witchcraft, and another the following year at Boston Common, and some eight more between then and 1692 in Connecticut and Massachusetts, but the great hysteria at Salem, where five men and 14 women were hanged, lasted but one year. The first hanged was Bridget Bishop, a feisty tavern owner disliked by the Puritans, who was accused of witchcraft earlier, in 1679. She, in fact, may have dabbled in the occult, but possibly only to frighten haughty neighbors. She was the only Salem witch hanged by herself. Usually, five accused of witchcraft were hanged together at Gallows Hill in Salem, except on September 22, 1692, when eight innocents convicted as witches, were hanged. *"We deplore witchcraft, and all means must be taken to combat the devil and his works,"* cried Cotton Mather, and *"all means"* were taken, until 19 were hanged, one was crushed to death, and quite a few of the estimated 168 lingering in jails as accused witches, died of exposure, disease and malnutrition, or went insane. It is a classic example of the phrase, which most Puritans came to realize after this one year of terror, *"We have met the enemy, and it is us!"*

The guilt and shame of these Puritans, when they realized that their religious fanaticism and fear of Satan had caused such pain, agony and death, must have been overwhelming. Some, of course, like Cotton Mather, continued to believe that all those accused were *"expostulating with the devil,"* and that the witch hunt should continue. In fact, the law punishing witches in Massachusetts wasn't repealed until 1736. Attorney and author-historian, Samuel L. Knapp wrote in the 19th century of what followed the witch trials in Salem: *"After this troubled night of weakness and crime had passed away, its benefits were felt. The whole Community were sensible of the delusion which had governed them; the criminal code assumed milder features, and the administration of justice more lenient rules."*

The Essex Gazette of November 12, 1771, reveals just how guilt-ridden the people of Salem and its environs were after the 1692 witch-hysteria. The paper read that, *"Bryan Sheehan, convicted of rape, is the first person, as far as we can learn, that has been convicted of Felony, in this large County (of 34 villages and towns), since the memorable year 1692, commonly called 'Witch-Time.'"* Over 77 years without a felony in such a large heavily populated area, which includes everything north of Boston to the New Hampshire border, seems almost unbelievable. But, as these Puritans once feared witches, they now apparently feared hurting their fellow man. Even if someone committed a crime, it seems that the people of Essex County, and especially Salem, would not convict. They had obviously had their fill of crime and punishment in 1692. The tide turned again, however, in 1772 at the notorious little town called Salem – a name Governor Endicott gave the place in 1626, a name which in Hebrew means *"peace."*

Young Bryan Sheehan had raped Abigail Hollowell, wife of Ben Hollowell of neighboring Marblehead. There were mitigating circumstances, such as that it may have been adultery rather than rape, under which circumstance Abigail would have faced the hangman, and not Bryan. This, of course, was before lawyers began assisting the accused, and since Bryan was Irish Catholic, which was a strike against him in the land of the Puritans, he was convicted. On the cold, frosty morning of January 16, 1772, Bryan was carried in a cart, sitting on his handmade wooden coffin, the mile from Salem Jail to Winter Island, a neck of land connected to the mainland by a narrow road. It had been decided for some unknown reason not to hang him at the legendary Gallows Hill where the Salem witches were hanged. In spite of the chill and the lengthy time lapse since the last Salem hanging, an estimated 12,000 people showed up at Winter Island to watch the show. Besides Sheehan, on the macabre billing was a mulatto named George, who sat on the newly constructed gallows with a noose around his neck for an hour. Then his shirt was stripped off his back and he was whipped 20 stripes in front of the crowd. George had been involved in some sort of a brawl in Gloucester, for which he was supposed to get 39 stripes of the whip, but the governor, apparently pleased that hanging was alive again north of Boston, remitted 19 stripes. Bryan noticeably trembled as he stood before the hangman. Those in the audience were trembling, too, from the cold and the winter wind blowing off the water, but they seemed jovial enough. All the good things to eat at the makeshift refreshment stands were sold out before the day was over. There was a groan, almost in unison, as Bryan Sheehan was dropped to dangle at the end of his rope, his body twitching for many minutes thereafter. It was a good afternoon of entertainment. There wasn't a sign of guilt or shame in the crowd from those *"Witch Times."* To attract a crowd of 12,000 in the middle of winter to a windswept island, his hanging was obviously filling some deep dark void within their black souls. Like the young female accusers of Salem in 1692, *"We must have some sport,"* was their cry.

There wasn't another hanging at Winter Island, Salem for fifteen years, and apparently this instilled a pride in some, for the <u>Massachusetts Gazette</u> of December 1786 read: *"This is the only execution which had taken place in the County of Essex for nearly 15 years, and but the second since about the close of the last century. The concourse of people was consequently great – and the conduct of the military corps was highly applauded."* The subject of all the excitement was Isaac Cooms, age 39, a mulatto – half Negro and half Indian. He had killed his wife. On the chilly morning of the execution, two days before Christmas, Isaac was escorted in chains to Salem's Tabernacle Church, where such a crowd had gathered that most could not fit into the church. The sermon by Reverend Spalding was, we are told, *"well adapted to the melancholy occasion,"* and the prisoner, who was made to face the crowd during the sermon, was then returned to the jail until two o'clock in the afternoon. Isaac was then seated in the back of an open, horse-drawn cart, and led to the *"Execution Hill"* at Winter Island by the High Sheriff who was on horseback. The Sheriff was surrounded by 40 constables and deputies carrying pikes. People along the wayside cheered and booed as the procession passed, and as they reached Winter Island Road, the crowd grew larger and more boisterous. As was the case at Sheehan's hanging, there were well over 12,000 spectators in attendance, more than twice the population of Salem itself. The cart was rolled under the specially erected gallows, and the noose was placed around Isaac Cooms' neck. Reverend Hopkins offered a prayer, which quieted the crowd, and then Isaac was asked if he had any last words. Cooms had prepared a farewell address, which he had the minister read:

"I who has been called Isaac Cooms, but my right name is John Peters. I have been a traveler ever since, til I now arrived to this unhappy place....My advice is to all spectators to refrain from lying, stealing and all suchlike things, but in particular not to break the Sabbath of the Lord, or game at cards, or get drunk, as I have done. This is my advice, and more in particular, to mixt coulard people and youths of every kind...Amen." Isaac bowed his head, the cart was led off, and he was left there hanging. There were no cheers or boos. As one eyewitness reporter concluded: *"The unhappy sufferer made the expiation which the law required for his horrid and unnatural crime. His behavior, through the whole, was firm, but decent, penitent and devotional."* Everyone then left the hanging scene to celebrate Christmas.

Coincidentally, a year later, another Sheehan named John was hanged at Boston Common for burglary on November 22, 1787. Ironically, only a few years after that, another man named Cooms – George Cooms, also faced the hangman for killing his wife in Boston. There were many eye witnesses to the murder, who saw it through the cracks of the house. It was winter and George and Maria Cooms started yelling and screaming at each other about who would gather wood to make a fire in the fireplace. Neighbors were aroused by the yelling, and peeked into the drafty living room through cracks in the clapboards. They saw George Cooms kick his wife many times and then jump on her, which seemed to be the blow that killed her. George Cooms was arrested and imprisoned, to be brought to trial before a jury a few weeks later. In testimony it was emphasized that George had been a hero, a gunner aboard the invincible battleship U.S.S. CONSTITUTION – *"Old Ironsides."* George Cooms was found not guilty

– the jury was made up of Revolutionary War veterans. There was a similar result in 1806, when Thomas Selfridge shot Charles Austin in an age-old Boston family feud. Selfridge had published a notice in the Boston newspaper, which read that, *"Austin is a coward, liar, and scoundrel."* Austin then went to Selfridge's house to club him with his cane, but he never got a chance, for Selfridge expected him and shot him in cold blood. Like George Cooms, Selfridge had been a war veteran. He was found guilty of only *"self-defense,"* and thereby avoided the hangman – on the jury was America's beloved patriot, Paul Revere. Paul certainly wouldn't have wanted to see an old war compatriot hang.

As patriotic fervor obviously saved George Cooms and Thomas Selfridge, it also resulted in the hanging of an innocent, unborn child at Brookfield, Massachusetts in 1778. It was a cold March evening as farmer Joshua Spooner walked the two miles home from Cooley's Inn. Half-way there, three men jumped him, clubbing and knifing him to death, then dropped him into a nearby well. Within a week, the three murderers were seen in and around the village wearing Spooner's clothes, which were easily recognized by the local people who knew Spooner well. The three men, Brooks, Buchanan and Ross, were Army deserters, and to make matters worse, Buchanan had been a British Redcoat. These men were wearing, among other things, Spooner's belt buckle, his favorite winter coat, and his pocket watch. Although Joshua Spooner hadn't been reported missing by his beautiful young wife, Bathsheeba, he hadn't been seen by anyone in days. The three deserters were arrested by the local constables, and when grilled on how they obtained Joshua's belongings, Ezra Ross broke down and confessed. He led the constables and sheriff to the well where the body was deposited. The well water had frozen, and Spooner lay on top of the ice. All three murderers then confessed that they had been paid $1,000 to kill Spooner by his wife, Bathsheeba. At first, the authorities wouldn't believe the deserters. She was, after all, a devoted wife and mother, the daughter of famous General Tim Ruggles, who at that moment was suffering with George Washington and his men at Valley Forge. The evidence against her, however, was overwhelming, and she was arrested. Before her desired counsel, Levi Lincoln, arrived on the scene, she confessed to planning the murder of her husband and hiring the three deserters to attack him. Levi Lincoln, probably for the first time in American legal history, pleaded before the Worcester County Court that Bathsheeba Spooner was insane and didn't know what she was doing when she hired the men. *"She was and is of unsound and distracted mind,"* Lincoln told the judge and jury. *"The whole evidence is that of a fool. She was born in high rank of life, well educated and an accomplished wife and mother, and in the enjoyment of good estate, what object would she have in undertaking such a detestable crime?....After the murder, she gave the murderers his watch, his buckles, waistcoat, breeches, shirts, and even had them put the items on, to be worn in the eyes of the world, where they were well known to be Spooner's clothes. Was this the conduct of a person in the exercise of reason?"* The General's mind was also shattered upon hearing what his daughter had done. He not only left the Army, but America as well, and like the hated Tories, sought asylum in Canada. The insanity plea didn't work for Bathsheeba Ruggles Spooner, but another plea was made prior to her scheduled hanging in Worcester on July 2nd. Reverend Thanes MacCarthy revealed that Bathsheeba was pregnant. This also was dismissed by the judge as a ploy to save the murderess, and with her three co-conspirators, she was hanged before a jovial crowd of over 5,000 in the midst of a terrible thunderstorm. In the eyes of the authorities, *"she died poorly,"* spitting and screaming, struggling in the rain against the hangman in every way she could. She, of course, was struggling for two. Hers was a last desperate attempt to have them save her unborn child, but its innocent life was also snuffed out by the hangman. The thunderstorm had put somewhat of a damper on the spirits of those present at the hanging of the pregnant woman and the three deserters, but there had been many wild parties and parades through the Worcester streets the night before, so that not all the joviality had been lost by the wind and rain.

In 1788, there was a double hanging on Boston Common on the Fourth of July, and there was a gala concert torch light procession in the evening, all of which added some spice to the holiday. Often magistrates would purposely schedule hangings on holidays to add to the festivities. There was great disappointment in Boston in 1817, when wife killer William McDonald was slated to hang on December 26th, but unexpectedly died of a heart attack before hanging day. At the same time in England, where hangings were also a main source of entertainment, Elizabeth Godfrey was being hanged at Newgate for stabbing one Richard Prince to death. As a second and third featured attraction to the day's festivities, two Irishmen, Owen Haggerty and John Holloway, were scheduled to be hanged as well, for their crimes of robbery. The hangmen was known to be a sloppy executioner, which attracted a larger audience, for the victims would twitch and struggle for a longer period of time at the end of their respective ropes. Elizabeth had been twitching for half an hour, as the seemingly mesmerized crowd looked on, when a pieman spilled some of the pies that he was selling near the gallows. When a few people bent over to help him pick them up, some boys gathered several pies up and ran off with them, causing others to trip over those assisting the pieman. It was like dominoes, and the crushing mob began stomping over those who had fallen. Everyone stopped watching the hanging, and tried to save themselves from being trampled or crushed. When order was restored, there were heaps of bodies strewn about the hanging platform. Many injured had to be taken off to the hospital – but 42 spectators had been stomped to death. A similar near-tragedy occurred on New Year's Day, 1776, when twins were hanged together at the notorious Tyburn Gallows. Robert and Daniel Perreau, local businessmen, were convicted as forgers and slated to hang at the snow-covered gallows. Along with them, *"two nameless ragged Jews, for housebreaking,"* were also scheduled to hang. It was advertised as *"The biggest Tyburn Fair since Lord Ferrers was hanged."* At Tyburn, authorities boasted, there was room on the gallows for twelve to be hanged at once. The Jews were hanged first as a preliminary, and then the twins, holding hands. This provided such an exciting main event that the crowd pushed forward with too much enthusiasm, almost tipping the cart that the victims stood in, crushing many women and children in the first row of spectators. The Army restored order, as those who were injured or had fainted in the crush were carried away through the snow on sledges and sleds. The show then continued on as scheduled, as though nothing had happened, and the twins *"swung side by side, their hands clasped together for nearly a minute.*

Then, when they drifted into unconsciousness their clasped hands slowly parted." It was a unique double feature.

The celebration of a hanging, especially if it occurred as part of a regularly scheduled holiday, often began the day before and continued well into the eve of the event. One noted writer of the 1800s, experiencing a pre-hanging celebration for the first time, was not pleasantly surprised: *"When I came upon the scene at midnight, the shrillness of the cries and howls that were raised from time to time, denoting they came from a concourse of boys and girls already assembled in the best places, made my blood run cold. As the night went on, screeching, laughing, and the yelling in strong chorus of the parodies of Negro melodies with the substitution of Mrs. Manning (the woman being hanged) for Oh Susannah were added to these. When day dawned, thieves, low prostitutes, ruffians and vagabonds of every kind, flocked to the ground with every variety of offensive and foul behavior. Fighting, fainting, whistling, brutal jokes, tumultuous demonstrations of indecent delight when swooning women were dragged out of the crowd by police with their dresses disordered, gave a new zest to the general entertainment..."* Thus were the observations of Charles Dickens.

Counterfeiters, forgers, highwaymen and pirates were, by far ,the favorites of the hanging-watchers, for they were hardly ever repentant, and they often gave rebellious, irreverent, and sometimes funny speeches before they swung into eternity. Jack Quelch, commander of a pirate crew out of Marblehead, was marched to the gallows in escort of forty armed men at Boston on June 30, 1704. He strutted the gallows platform where, Judge Sewall informs us, *"The river was covered with people in a hundred boats and canoes,"* and on shore there were thousands more. Quelch waved and bowed to his audience, as if on stage. *"I am not afraid of death,"* he shouted to them, *"but I am afraid of what follows."* He laughed and joked, and concluded by saying, *"I am condemned only upon circumstances, but all should take care how they bring money into New England – they could be hanged for it."* Another notorious pirate, William Fly, also condemned to die at Boston in July of 1726, said, as he marched to the gallows with a flower clutched in his hand, *"tell all that I died a brave fellow."* He greeted all along the way with a smile and a nod, like a politician campaigning for office, and he was still smiling when the noose was placed around his neck. His body, like Quelch's, was gibbeted in chains, as most bodies of pirates were. Nix's Mate was the spot, a little island in Boston Harbor, where all mariners could see his flesh rot and bones drop from the chains as they cruised in and out of the harbor. This ghastly scene, like public hangings, authorities decided, was also a deterrent to crime. Charles Marchant, sentenced to be hanged as a pirate on December 18, 1826, at Boston, shouted at the judge and jury, *"What? Is that what you brought me here for, to tell me I must die? No thank you!"* Marchant managed to hang himself in his cell the day before he was to hang on the gallows. Two Maine men, Peter Williams and Abraham Cox, were hanged for piracy in the jail yard before a large crowd at Auburn on August 27, 1858. A poem on a broadbill was read by Williams before the noose was placed around his neck. It read in part:

> *"On Saint Martin Island I was born,*
> *Twelve years was I a slave;*
> *My mistress she was kind to me*
> *And to me my freedom gave.*
> *Soon after that I went to sea*
> *On the Southern coast did sail,*
> *Four years I went before the mast,*
> *Then withstood the roughest gale.*
> *Seamen when you're treated harsh,*
> *You'd better bear the pain;*
> *If you resist you'll suffer more,*
> *And nothing will you gain.*
> *I've suffered much to ills of life,*
> *Til my years are sixty-eight;*
> *With crippling limbs and tottering frame,*
> *I'm led to gallows gate..."*

Noted pirate Henry Phillips, who came from a long line of pirates, was sentenced to hang for killing Gaspard Denegri at Roebuck Tavern, Boston, in March of 1817. When he stood on the gallows, with a white cap drawn over his eyes, he sang a song and then dropped his handkerchief, which was the signal for the hangman to drop the trapdoor to let him swing. Exactly 45 years later, on March 8, 1862, the last New England pirate was hanged. His name was Captain Nathaniel Gordon, and his last words were, *"Goodnight, sweet prince,"* which surely would have pleased Shakespeare.

The most loved criminals of the 19th century were the highwaymen, in England as well as New England. They were inevitably compared to Robin Hood and the beloved *"cool, calm and collected"* Ben Turpin, who joked at the hanging tree as he was being executed for horse thievery in 1739. He set the pace for the gallant highwaymen to come. All highwaymen in Europe seemed to have aliases: *"Captain Lightfoot"* and *"Captain Thunderbolt"* were the most famous, and these two were considered heroes by the general public of Britain . As young gentlemen robbers, they waylaid stagecoaches, taking from the rich and giving to the poor, and stealing naught from women but a kiss. They were both close to being captured in 1817 in England, but then disappeared, never to be seen again in the British Isles. They came to New England, Thunderbolt to Vermont and Lightfoot to Massachusetts. Thunderbolt *"went straight "* and became a doctor, but although Michael Martin, alias Captain Lightfoot, tried to live a normal life, he failed and fell back into his old profession. A master of disguise, Captain Lightfoot would often dress as a priest or minister, visiting wedding receptions, where he would rob all the guests of their valuables at gun point, but allowed the bride to keep her new ring. He had been known to mask himself as a woman, although he was a husky, giant of a man. He would ride sidesaddle along the heavily traveled roads, purposely falling off his horse. When gentlemen stopped to help the *"lady"* in distress, he would rob them. He met his match in Major John Bray, whom he stopped coming from a governor's party on the Medford Road, stealing his watch. Bray immediately organized a posse and chased Michael Martin on horseback. In Springfield, he startled him in his hotel bed and dragged him all the way back to Cambridge, where he was jailed. Michael was well aware of the little poem about Cambridge, and found it most fitting to his circumstance:

"Cambridge is famous,
Both for wit and knowledge.
Some they whip and some they hang,
And some they send to college."

Michael Martin was an extremely witty and intelligent man, but he knew he wasn't in Cambridge to attend Harvard. When the judge pronounced his sentence of death by hanging, he replied, *"Well, your honor, that's the worst you can do for me."* Martin almost managed to escape on the morning of December 8, 1821, and although he broke out of the East Cambridge jail, he was captured in a nearby cornfield, where he beat up three guards before he was subdued. His nickname thereafter was *"the merry strongman."* He smiled and joked with the crowd as he was escorted by an army of men to the gallows. The hangman was so nervous, as his victim was so jovial, that he couldn't get the noose over Martin's head. Martin had to do it for him. He had the crowd laughing lustily, telling one joke after another and making fun of his own predicament. Looking at the two black horses leading a wagon that carried his coffin, he shouted in his finest Irish brogue, *"Ah look now, I have a private carriage to take me into eternity."* The crowd laughed, Michael dropped his handkerchief, the trap door fell open, and he dropped to his death, a roguish grin still creasing his face.

Counterfeiters, or *"coiners,"* as they were called, and forgers, were second class citizens when it came to hanging. They were not driven to the gallows in a horse-drawn cart like all the others, but were dragged to the gallows or hanging tree either on a leather mat or a horse-drawn sledge of oxhide. This resulted in most of them being half dead when they met the hangman. The reason for this was that forgers and coiners were considered the most detestable criminals, for their crimes often affected entire communities and sometimes colonies, where their counterfeit coins or bills could ruin or near-ruin the local economy. They were known to have been beaten up by mobs on the way to the gallows. Counterfeiting was considered an act of treason by New England authorities until 1829, when Thomas Maynard, the last to hang as a traitor for counterfeiting, was executed. Yet, New England had more than its fair share of counterfeiters, including William Scott of Salem, John David of Boston, Joseph Boyle of Lynn, Owen Sullivan of New Hampshire, and Gilbert Belcher of Connecticut, all noted 18th century con-men who made their own money. Of all, the cleverest and most successful was Sullivan. He was first arrested at Boston in 1750 on testimony from his drunken wife, who called him *"a forty thousand pound money maker."* He was found guilty of passing false bills, spent a day in the pillory and received forty lashes. Two years later, he was caught making and passing near-perfect 16-pound notes at Providence, Rhode Island, where he again ended up in the pillory. This time, however, he had both ears cropped, and the letter *"C"* branded into his right cheek with a red-hot poker. After spending a few weeks in the Providence jail, he escaped north to Nottingham, New Hampshire, where he organized an elaborate distribution network throughout New England and New York, which he called *"The Dover Money Club."* All 60 or so members distributed counterfeit pound-notes throughout the colonies. An estimated 20,000 pound-notes were made from his plates at Nottingham. By 1755, 20 of his club members had been caught. Four of his gang captured in Newport admitted to making and spending over 50,000 pounds (an estimated $100,000) from Owen Sullivan's money plates. The authorities placed a bounty for capture, dead or alive, on *"Sullivan the Scoundrel's"* head. Connecticut law enforcer, Eliphalet Beacher, with a bunch of his relatives, began a crusade to track Sullivan down. After a few months of hunting, they captured Sullivan hiding in the house of a friend. He was to hang in April of 1756, but his friends chopped down the gallows with axes, and it had to be rebuilt. On May 10th, Sullivan appeared before a large crowd at the newly restored gallows. He took a big bite into a plug of chewing tobacco and said: *"I urge my friends to quit coining, but I ain't gonna tell you who those friends are...I won't tell you how many bills I had printed, and I won't tell you where they are. You'll have to find that out by your own learning."* He nodded to the hangman, smiled to the crowd, swallowed his tobacco, and was hanged. When it came time for his Connecticut compatriot, silversmith Gilbert Belcher, to experience the same fate eight years later, he told the crowd that, *"No gain afforded me so much pleasure as that I acquired by illicit means."*

A highwayman, a counterfeiter, and a murderer – William Daneesse, William Smith, and Rachel Wall – the subjects of a triple hanging slated for Boston Common on October 24, 1789, drew the largest audience ever – an estimated 20,000. Most were interested in 29 year old Rachel, a beautiful woman who claimed she was innocent of the crime she was about to hang for. She had been a parlor maid on Beacon Hill, but was caught red-handed stealing valuables from the cabin of a vessel docked at the waterfront. In the same boat, a sailor was found dead in his bunk and Rachel was accused and later convicted of his murder – he had been stabbed to death. Up until the moment she climbed the ladder to the gallows platform, she shouted to the crowd that she was innocent of the sailor's murder. This aroused many in the crowd who persuaded the hangman to allow her to speak. Rachel, standing before the crowd with the noose about her neck, convinced everyone there that she was innocent of her crime – she had not killed the sailor. She had, however, she told them, murdered some 24 men from 1781 to 1782, when she and her husband had pirated twelve vessels off Portsmouth, New Hampshire, stealing many valuables and over $6,000 in cash. She would stand at the mast of her husband's sailing smack, pretending she was in distress, and when other sailors stopped to help, she and her husband would kill them. When she finished her confession, the hangman did his duty and hanged her for a murder she did not commit. Rachel was the last woman hanged in Massachusetts.

The death penalty for women who killed their newborn children, usually because they were illegitimate, was in effect as a law in New England until the early 20th century. More women were hanged for this crime in New England than any other, but most executions for infanticide, as they called it, occurred in the 17th and 18th centuries. It also wasn't unusual in those days for judges to hang children for such minor offenses as stealing chickens or shoplifting. The last public hanging for arson in New England was of Stephen Clark of Newburyport, Massachusetts, for torching a barn in October of 1820, when he was 15 years old. Although he pleaded not guilty, he was convicted, but delayed at the Essex County Jail for over a year and a half until he turned 17. At that time, he was marched off to Execution Hill, Winter Island, Salem, and hanged in front of a large cheering crowd. The Children's Act of 1908 did away with the execution of children under 16 years of age, and a few years later the law was changed to exclude all those under 18 years of age. It was shortly after Stephen Clark's hanging that the execution of criminals was moved indoors in Massachusetts, away from the general public. In some jurisdictions, a small gathering of onlookers was allowed behind the jail walls to witness a hanging in the jailyard, but in many places hangings became a private affair inside the jail, completely eliminating the macabre holiday atmosphere.

Some American states, such as Montana and Washington, still offer hanging to the condemned as a death row option, and New Hampshire didn't remove hanging from the books until January 1st, 1991. Lethal injection is now the capital punishment of choice for the Granite State. The last official hanging in New England was at Concord, New Hampshire on July 14, 1939. Howard Long was hanged at the prison for the murder of ten-year-old Mark Jensen at Laconia, New Hampshire in 1937. The last public hanging in New England was also in New Hampshire, on May 6, 1868. Samuel Mills, a farm laborer, killed his employer, George Maxwell of Franconia, with an axe, with the intent of robbing him of all his money. The old farmer had hid his money well however, and Mills couldn't find it, so he hopped a train west. Boston detectives were hard on his heels, and Mills was captured in Illinois and brought back to New Hampshire. Days before he was to hang, Mills was displayed at the local tavern for the people of Franconia to see. Even school was let out, so that children could question the murderer about his evil deed. Mills, wearing leg shackles, was kept at the Haverhill jail rather than in Concord and twice escaped and was recaptured before his scheduled hanging date. It was an exciting day in the village of Haverhill on this sunny May morning, with some 3,000 people on hand to witness the hanging, and an expected 500 more coming on a special train from Concord. A young eye-witness, Elmore Whipple of Franconia, explained that the gallows itself was nothing more than *"a rough hemlock joist projecting six feet from the windows of Mills' cell on the second floor of the jail...in full view of the street...Near the center of the gallows floor the trap was arranged; beneath it the earth was removed to give a fall of nine feet...At about 10 o'clock, Sheriff Stevens, his deputies, legal advisors, and newspaper reporters ascended the platform. There was a lot of criticism in the crowd about this, for some folks didn't think it fair that the trainload from Concord, which still had not arrived, should be cheated out of the sight of the hanging. Mills reached the platform through the window. He was laced in a white canvas bag...He took his place over the drop. The death warrant was read and a prayer was offered."*

"Mr. Mills, you have 20 minutes longer to live. Is there anything you wish to say?" asked the sheriff.

"I bid farewell to this world," shouted Mills so all could hear. *"Tell the people that Samuel Mills died like a man."*

The sheriff, looking at his pocket watch, then shouted, *"You now have fifteen minutes to live...Now ten...Now five...Now one...Now you have no more time Mr. Mills, may God have mercy on your soul."*

"Good-bye, gentlemen." Mills managed to cry out before he dropped through the door to dangle in mid-air.

Elmore Whipple informs us that after the hanging, *"I couldn't eat lunch, and all I wanted to do was go home. That was the only hanging I ever saw, and I never wanted to see another."* Neither do we.

Captain Lightfoot

Old sketch of the hanging of Michael Martin at Charlestown, Massachusetts. He was the notorious, but loved, highwayman Captain Lightfoot.

Woodcut of the hanging of Rachel Wall on Boston Common in 1789, with two others. 20,000 came to see Rachel, who swore that she didn't murder the sailor she was accused of stabbing to death, but she did admit that she was a pirate. The sheriff hanged her for murder anyway.

Hanging of murderer Samuel Mills at Haverhill, New Hampshire in 1868 (he's the one dressed in white.) This was New England's last public hanging.
Photo courtesy of the New Hampshire Historical Society.

Crowds gathered at Gallows Hill, Salem, for the hanging of witches in 1692. Nineteen in all were hanged that year, all innocent victims.
From the television series, "Three Sovereigns for Sarah," Nightowl Productions, Martha's Vineyard, MA. Photo of hanging by Mikki Ansin.

IV

Burning, Boiling and Beheading

Barbara Spencer was a young beautiful girl. She left home one day to witness a public hanging and never returned. Her parents knew that she had run off, for she had long been unmanageable and belligerent toward them, even before she reached her teens. She had met new friends in the crowd at the hanging, and she had gone off to live with them – they were counterfeiters, and she began assisting them in distributing their false money. She was soon discovered and arrested. At court, her friends were acquitted, but Barbara, on May 11, 1721, was found guilty and sentenced to death by burning at the stake. The local newspaper reported that, *"While under sentence of death she behaved in the most indecent and turbulent manner; nor could she be convinced that she had been guilty of any crime in making a few shillings. She was for some time very impatient under the idea of her approaching dissolution, and was particularly shocked at the thought of being burnt..."*

Five years later, almost to the day, May 9, 1726, Catherine Hayes was publicly burned at the stake for the murder of her husband. The hangman, who performed all such tasks as whipping, beheading, burning and other tortures and killings, was supposed to personally strangle Mrs. Hayes while she was chained at the stake, before the firewood was lit under her feet. He forgot, and the fire was lit. Apparently the officials of the 18th century considered that strangling a woman almost to death before burning her to a crisp was an act of kindness. The hangman, seeing his mistake, tried to quickly strangle Mrs. Hayes as the fire progressed, but he only scorched his own hands in the attempt, and he quickly backed away. Mrs. Hayes screeched as the flames licked her legs and she tried to kick away the burning wood. Some witnesses said that she screamed for almost thirty minutes as she slowly roasted. Usually crowds witnessing an execution were jovial and brazen, but this crowd was silent and horror-stricken.

Seven years later there was another public burning. This time it was Elizabeth Wright, a pretty counterfeiter. The newspaper reported that *"she was put up in the cart with other prisoners and joined in the prayers and*

73

when the prayers were over begged hard to be hanged with them. She was afterwards fastened to the stake set up on purpose and burned to ashes but was dead before the flames touched her, the executioner having first thrown down the stool on which she stood from under her feet, and given her several blows on the breast."

Three years later, a young servant girl from Lynn was burned at the stake for allowing a murderer to come into the house of her employer, even though it was never proven beyond a shadow of a doubt that she had left the door open on purpose. This horrible execution did not happen in Lynn, Massachusetts, but in Lynn, England, and the others aforementioned here were also in England and not New England. Many believe that burning at the stake was never practiced here in New England, however, history proves that some were burned here. At about the time the Pilgrims and Puritans were settling in, the Episcopalians of England were burning Anabaptists, strangling and cutting out the bowels of Catholics, and hanging Puritans. Witches were either drowned in a muddy swamp, *"by the Queen's special grace,"* or were burned at the stake. But Cotton Mather decided he preferred hanging witches, for burning, he said, *"is an invention of Catholics and Episcopalians."*

It was called *"pethy treason"* when a wife murdered her husband, and the punishment was to be burned alive. This lasted until 1790 in England, *"after which, on June 5,"* Parliament decided, *"women will suffer hanging like men."* Women, it seems, for centuries, were given the special privilege of burning at the stake. The last time a person was burned at the stake in New England was on September 18, 1755 at Charlestown, Massachusetts. The public seemed to prefer burning at the stake over drowning and hanging, for it was a slower and more agonizing punishment for the convicted, but burning corpses give off a distinctive foul smell, and it made many people sick. Yet, when it was discontinued as a punishment, the authorities announced that *"women under sentence of death should not be burned, burning being an inhuman punishment."* All those burned at the stake in New England were African-Americans.

At Roxbury, Massachusetts in 1681, a black slave named Maria burned down the house of her master Joshua Lamb, and she was burned at the stake for doing it. Another African slave named Jack, from Northampton, Massachusetts, while scrounging to find something to eat in the home of his master William Clark, accidentally set the house afire. He was taken in chains to Roxbury where he was hanged at the gallows until he was almost dead and then he joined Maria. He was chained to a stake beside her and burned with her in the same fire in 1681. Yet, in 1735, two Afro-American slaves, Yaw and Caesar of Boston, attempted to poison their master my mixing arsenic into his breakfast chocolate. The two were discovered. Their master, Mr. Humphrey Scarlett, became violently ill, but didn't die. The penalty for poisoning was burning at the stake, but old man Yaw and Caesar, who was only a boy, were merely whipped. Slaves living in and around the Boston area at that time were also familiar with the story of an evil New England slave-owner named Ben Salmon, who was also poisoned with arsenic by two of his slaves. Salmon died in his sleep, and no one but the Afro-Americans were the wiser on the real reason for his death, and all of Salmon's human holdings were sold away to kinder and gentler owners. This fairy tale-like ending to the murder of a mean master, set the stage for one of the most well known murder mysteries in Colonial history.

Phillis, Phoebe and Mark were three slaves owned by a fairly wealthy saddler named John Codman of Charlestown. Phillis, a young woman who had been with Codman since she was bought at the slave market as a child, hated her master. Phoebe and Mark were married and purchased by Codman in 1749. They also thought Codman was too strict. Mark, in fact, set his master's workshop on fire that year, hoping he might be angry enough to sell him and his wife to someone else, but Mark was whipped as a penalty and not sold away to a kinder master. Within a few years, Mark and the women could take no more, so they conspired to kill Codman. All three had been converted to Christianity and Mark could read and write. He read over the Bible, looking for a loophole that might allow him to commit murder in this life without a penalty for doing it in the next. He decided that if he killed without bloodshed, it was not a major sin, and of course, there were those Boston slaves that got away with poisoning their master only a few years back. So Mark convinced Phillis and Phoebe that they should poison Mr. Codman.

Mark persuaded his friend Robin, another slave who worked in the apothecary shop of a Doctor Clark, to steal him some arsenic. Robin later insisted that he thought Mark wanted the poison to kill pigs. *"Two quarts would make them swell right up,"* he said, but Captain Codman didn't *"swell right up."* Phillis and Phoebe added the poison to his morning gruel and barley water, and mixed it with his chocolate, as Yaw and Caesar of Boston had done, but Codman didn't even get sick. He seemed to thrive on the arsenic added to his diet. Phillis and Phoebe thought it was funny that Codman didn't even get sick and they giggled about it when Codman left the house. Mark returned to Robin for more arsenic – a stronger dosage this time. After drinking his final cup of chocolate laced with arsenic, Captain Codman writhed in pain for fifteen hours before he died, and the slaves danced with joy, but the joy was short lived. Upon questioning the slaves about Codman's death, Phillis became hysterical and confessed, then turned state's evidence. She was shipped off to the West Indies to be re-sold as a slave. Mark was convicted of murder, and Phoebe was convicted of pethy treason, thus to be burned at the stake.

In the early afternoon of September 18, 1755, at Cambridge, Massachusetts, a large crowd came to watch Mark hang. That done, ten feet away from the gallows, Phoebe was placed on a stool with a rope around her neck, and tied to a stake surrounded by twigs, wood and straw. The hangman then kicked away the stool, causing her to fall into the pile of wood and be strangled by the noose. Before she died, the fire was lit and she was burned to a crisp.

Two days later, there was a short article in the <u>Boston Evening Post,</u> which read: *"Thursday last, in the afternoon, Mark, a Negro man, and Phillis, a Negro woman, both servants of the late John Codman, were executed at Cambridge, for poisoning their said Master. The fellow was hanged, and the woman burned at the stake about ten yards distant from the gallows. They both confessed themselves guilty of the crime for which they suffered, acknowledged the justice of their sentence, and died very*

76

penitent. After execution, the body of Mark was brought down to Charlestown Common and hanged in chains on a Gibbet erected there for that purpose."

Mark remained hanging in chains on the Cambridge Road, now Washington Street, for over twenty years. After a few years, he shriveled up into a ghastly looking mummy, where crows and blackbirds often fluttered to pick at his dried skin and bones. Young boys were often taken there to see the corpse by their fathers, as a lesson of what happens to those who commit crime. Among the boys who mention seeing the body of *"Black Mark"* as children were patriots Paul Revere and John Hancock. Paul mentions him again on the night of his famous midnight ride in 1775, for it was where a patrol of British Army officers intercepted him. He didn't call it Charlestown Common – he described it as *"Where Mark's body hung in chains."* A place that had frightened him as a little boy and apparently still did on the night of his heroic ride. Gibbeting criminals then, we might conclude, seemed to have the desired results.

Gibbeting is an offshoot of boiling a person to death, which was a legal punishment in England in the 16th century. In 1542, a woman named Margaret Davy was boiled alive in a large pot of hot oil at Lynn for poisoning Richard Coke, a local minister. A common punishment for a traitor was to be fastened in chains and dunked into an iron pot filled with hot oil several times, until dead. The reason this punishment didn't last is that it took several hours to get the oil to boil during which time the spectators became impatient. Boiling water replaced the oil, and a few traitors were publicly cooked, but it too required much preparation and was also time consuming. To save time, toward the end of the century, condemned traitors were first chopped up, placed in the boiling pot, then hanged, the mutilated body finally discarded in a ditch. It was decided to reverse the process in the 17th century, hang them first, or have the hangman strangle them, then boil them to preserve the body so it could be displayed for a long time, chained near the site where their crime was committed. This was a common punishment in England and Scotland and not uncommon in early New England. The old English law of boiling alive, or even boiling them for gibbeting, is not known to have occurred in

New England, but, *"saturating the body with tar before it be hung in chains, in order that it might last longer,"* was common practice. *"Waving in the weather while his neck will hold,"* was an old Yankee expression that originated with the practice of gibbeting corpses of criminals. The rotting, stinking mummified corpses swayed on chains for years until they blew down or turned to dust to be swept away in a storm. No one dared unchain a gibbeted corpse, for fear of reprisal, but also for fear of evil spirits that supposedly always hovered about these macabre spectacles. Birds sometimes built their nests in a gibbeted man's skull, as was the case of an Indian hung in the gibbets at Boston Common in 1670, *"for murdering Zachary Smith in Dedham Woods."* And so, the little children playing on the Common would recite:

"There were nine tongues within one head,
The tenth went out to seek some bread,
To feed the living in the dead."

Many New England pirates, after being captured, jailed, found guilty and hanged, were then gibbeted. Usually chained to a ten or twelve-foot stake on an island or spit of land, where all entering or leaving a harbor would have a good view of them. The most popular spot for gibbeting pirates was Nix's Mate Island in Boston Harbor. Probably the most noted pirate gibbeted there was William Fly, a notorious sea-robber and barbarian, who was finally captured off Portsmouth, New Hampshire and hanged in July of 1726. After a triple hanging, Fly and two of his buccaneer friends, Sam Cole and Henry Greenville, were carried in a boat to Nix's Mate. Cole and Greenville were buried on the tiny island, but Fly's body was coated with hot pitch, so it wouldn't fall apart too soon, and was suspended in chains, *"as a spectacle for the warning of others, especially sea-faring men."* Boats and barges filled with spectators sailed out often to see him for the next few months after he was gibbeted. Then, as The Boston Newsletter reported in 1730, *"the corpse rotted in its chains, and the wind now whistles through his bones."* Nix's Mate, once a high 13-acre island, is now only a 32-foot pyramid of stone topped with a beacon. The entire island slowly disappeared underwater in the 18th century. It was once known as Bird Island, but the first mate under a

Captain Nix of Boston, his story lost to history, was accused of piracy, hanged and gibbeted at the island. He swore he was not a pirate, and because he was innocent, so the legend goes, the island sank in protest.

The most famous pirate of all time was Captain Kidd, a New England privateersman turned pirate, but he too claimed to be an innocent man before he was hanged and gibbeted. His partner in crime was the Governor of Massachusetts and New Hampshire, Richard Coots, the Earl of Bellomont. Coots, who originally hired Kidd, enticed him into Boston and then had him captured in front of his own home and thrown into Boston Jail. Captain Kidd, with his Irish side-kick Darby Mullins, was transported to England. There, still pleading his innocence, Kidd was tried and convicted of murder. On May 23, 1701, he and Mullins were hanged. However, on the three hour trip from the jail to Execution Dock, overlooking the mud flats of the Thames River, he got so drunk from merry spectators feeding him liquor, that he could hardly stand. When he was hanged, the rope broke and he landed in knee-deep mud, still alive. He was pulled out of the mud, and over protest of the mob, he was hanged again, successfully. His body was then painted with tar and he was delivered down river to Tilbury Fort where his corpse was sealed into an iron cage, or *"iron suit,"* as they called it, to preserve the body from falling to pieces. This also prevented surgeons from stealing it for experimentation. Captain Kidd remained gibbeted there for many years, while his partner in piracy lived in style and wealth as Governor of New England. Justice prevailed, however, for Coots went nearly insane trying to find Captain Kidd's buried treasure, and it brought him to an early grave.

The old English custom of hanging was tempered considerably in 17th century New England. There were originally seven distinct procedures to an English hanging, which were to be followed without deviation in the days when torture was considered a fine art: First, *"The person shall be drawn or dragged to the gallows."* Second, *"The person shall be hanged at the gallows, but let down before he died."* Third, *"His bowels are to be taken out with a sharp knife."* Fourth, *"His bowels are to be burnt before his eyes."* Fifth, *"His head is to be cut off."* Sixth, *"His body is to be divided into four parts,"* and seventh, *"All body parts and the head shall be placed wherever the King directs."* This old English law was in effect when the Pilgrims and Puritans came to America. One would think that these pious new settlers, who left Europe to escape such cruelties, would never practice such inhumane and gruesome procedures. However, in the Great Indian War, they often came close to following this recipe. When Canonchet, Chief of the Narragansetts, was shot in the woods at Pawtucket, Rhode Island, his body was cut into four parts and burned. Then his head was delivered to the Governor of Connecticut at Hartford. When Puritan Ben Church cornered the great Metocomet, better known as King Phillip, of the Wampanoags at Mount Hope, Rhode Island, in 1676, he and his men shot him dead. Then, Metacomet's left hand was cut off and given as a gift to Puritan Governor Leverett at Boston, and his right hand was preserved in a bucket of rum to display for years thereafter. His feet were hacked off and delivered as a gift to the people of Providence, Rhode Island. His body was halved, then quartered and hung on a nearby tree. His head was cut off and brought to the Pilgrims of Plymouth, where it was carried around on a pole in a great celebration. Metacomet's head remained in Plymouth for 25 years. displayed on a tall and permanent pole in the middle of town. As a final insulting gesture to this great Indian chief, son of Massasoit, Increase Mather, president of Harvard College, climbed the pole and threw his jawbone to the ground. The jawbone smashed, as Mather, in a rage, cried, *"This King Philip was a blasphemous leviathan."* Thus, the genteel pity of our Pilgrim-Puritan ancestors.

New England Indians were also involved in beheadings, and when King Philip's War began in 1675, the heads of six Swansea Island farmers were found mounted on long poles at the Mass Bay-Rhode Island border, after an Indian attack on the village there. Scalping is a result of the Indian tradition of cutting off the head of an enemy killed in battle. It was also a tradition of the Celtics. Not only was it cumbersome to carry heads of enemies back to the home village after a battle, but carrying more than one or two heads became a heavy load. Therefore scalping, just taking the scalp and hair of the enemy as a trophy, became the custom. In recent diggings in the Alps of ancient Celtic homes, archaeologists discovered crude display cases attached to these buried ancient homes. It was in these stone display cases where Celtic warriors exhibited heads of the enemies procured in battle. Beheading in most ancient societies was considered an honorable death. For centuries, the noblemen of England preferred it to hanging, and the last to be beheaded there was the eighty year old Lord Lovat, who was a notorious rebel. He dropped his handkerchief to the ground when he wanted the axe man to do his duty in April of 1747. It was 13 years later that British nobleman, the fourth Earl of Ferrers, was convicted of murdering his steward, and begged the king that he be decapitated and not hanged. The Earl considered beheading a *"nobler death,"* and said *"the rope is degrading,"* but the King refused to chop off his head. Instead, King George III offered a compromise and the Earl was hanged at the Tower of London, not by a *"degrading rope"* but by his own silk scarf. Strangely enough, when Edward Despard was sentenced to die after being caught in a plot to kill George III, the King would not allow hanging or beheading, which was the penalty for rebellion and treason. Instead, he had Despard drawn and quartered – disemboweled before his own eyes, his entrails burned under his nose. He was then tied to two horses and pulled in opposite directions. Finally, his head was cut off and his body sliced into four parts. This torturous death was still on the books in Britain at the turn of the 20th century, but Despard was the last to experience it.

A New Englander who came close to going the way of Despard was a New Hampshire lad names Edward Gove, who opposed Royal Governor Edward Cranfield in 1683 and attempted to start an armed rebellion against him. Gove was found guilty of treason and was brought to London. There he faced the punishment of hanging until almost dead, watching his bowels being taken from his stomach and burned, and *"when yet still living, have his head cut off."* However, Gove pleaded for mercy and got it, spending only three years imprisoned in the Tower of London. He was then allowed to return to New Hampshire, where he lived as a quiet citizen and was a rebel no more.

It seems that kings and queens of merry old England were getting their heads cut off by the axe man, or *"headsman"* as they called him, in record numbers throughout the last few centuries. The notorious Henry VIII (1509-1547), had the heads of two of his six wives chopped off *"for adultery and treason."* His daughter Elizabeth, as Queen of England, had 25 heads roll, and between father and daughter, it's estimated that they executed, mostly by hanging, over 80,000 people. Hanging was definitely an English invention, and was definitely preferred as an end-all there. Yet, in Halifax, Yorkshire, England in the early 1600s, there was no experienced hangman to be found, so a local friar invented a machine, called the *"Halifax Machine,"* which cut off heads. By 1650, Yorkshire had used the machine fifty times. The Scots had a similar contraption called *"The Maiden,"* which lopped off the heads of 100 prominent Scots by 1710. It was some eighty years later that the French revived this beheading instrument for the Revolution, calling it the *"guillotine,"* after a local doctor who suggested its use. The heavy steel blade dropped between two grooved uprights, disposing of many heads of nobility in France. It was thought to provide a painless death, but it was very messy, and that was why the English and the New English preferred hanging or slow strangulation – there was no bloody mess in these methods.

When the head of a criminal or traitor was cut off it was usually attached to a long pole, which was also part of the ritual performed by the axe man or headsman. The headsman in reality was the hangman, who was ordered by the sheriff to do all nasty tasks concerning death and torture. One of the most notorious of hangmen was Jack Ketch, who served in England for twenty years. His name is still popular in Punch and Judy puppet shows. Over the years, his name has been bastardized by the English, however, for he was really a Frenchman named Jacquette, and a notorious butcher at cutting off heads. He even wrote and published a pamphlet defending his decapitations, complaining that, *"the victim moved, and therefore it took five hacks to get the head off."* When he axed the poor Duke of Monmouth, it not only took him four whacks at the back of his neck, but he had to finally use a knife to finish the job. Many hangmen who were occasionally called on to chop off a head, would often practice their trade on animals to perfect their style. During Elizabeth's reign, a sailor named Brandon Derrick, accused with twenty other sailors of rape, told the authorities that he would hang his 19 shipmates if he would be spared. Thus, he became England's first official public executioner, and it is from him that we get the word *"derrick,"* meaning a construction crane with a rope or cable tied to it for lifting. Derrick's assistant, his cousin Gregory Brandon, also traveled England as a professional head-cutter and hangman, and their descendants continued on for generations as executioners. In Ireland in the late 1700s, the executioner of Connaught was a large middle aged woman named *"Lady Betty."* It is said that she was terribly tough on women who were convicted of crimes in that district and was especially sloppy at cutting off heads.

In New England, prisoners were often called upon to act as hangmen, sometimes to kill their colleagues. More times than not, though, it was the local sheriff or deputy sheriff who was the executioner. Sometimes the sheriff didn't wear a mask or black hood in an attempt to hide his identity, as did the hangmen of England, for most in a village or town could recognize the sheriff, mask or no mask. Often sheriff and hangmen were called upon to whip or burn books that the Puritan authorities thought vulgar or irreverent. William Pinchon's book, *"The Meritorious Price of our Redemption,"* published in 1650, received a Massachusetts General Court book review that was quite critical. *"We detest and abhor many of the opinions and assertions therein as false,"* said the representatives, *"and we hereby condemn this book to be burned in the market place at Boston, by the common executioner."* Almost every year at Salem or Boston, a book was deemed *"heretical,"* and ordered burned at a public place, and sometimes it was whipped first. As late as 1754 at Connecticut, a book was *"whipt forty stripes, save one, and then burnt."* One wonders in retrospect if the sheriff or deputy felt foolish whipping a book, or burning one at the stake. On King Street in Boston, also in 1754, the sheriff was ordered to whip and burn a book – it's title, *"Monster of Monsters."* One wonders who the monsters really were.

Probably the most monstrous punishments, next to burning, boiling and beheading, were those imposed on accused persons who were not willing to plead guilt or innocence. One punishment was to starve to death a person who wouldn't plead one way or the other . Another punishment was to use painful thumbscrews, or rip off fingernails, one by one, until a plea was forthcoming. The English were also known to stone people to death who remained mute or refused to plead one way or the other, but the most popular punishment of all in England was crushing a person to death, or to the point where he was willing to confess. The reason that people refused to plead their guilt was that if they pleaded guilty or were found guilty, they would forfeit all they owned to the crown, and their children would get no inheritance. If they remained silent, their estate could be transferred to their family after they were executed. The most striking example of a person trying to beat this warped, unjust system, is that of 80-year-old Giles Corey, who was accused by young girls of being an evil wizard during the 1692 witch hysteria. When asked by the magistrates if he was a wizard, he refused to answer, knowing he'd be damned no matter what he said. For remaining silent, the witch-hanging judges of Salem imposed the English law of *"slow crushing under weights until a plea is forthcoming."* Giles was forced to lie down naked in a pit next to the Salem Jail, with a door placed over his chest and stomach. Under direction of Sheriff George Corwin, heavy rocks were piled onto the door, slowly crushing the old man. As loud as Corwin shouted for Giles Corey to confess or plead one way of the other, he received no answer. Corey knew that if he replied, the sheriff would pillage his home, as he had the homes of previously confessed innocent victims. Ironically, all who said they were guilty lost their property; those who said they were innocent were hanged. After hours of this torture, Giles Corey expired, and three days later, Sheriff Corwin hanged his wife Martha at Salem's Gallows Hill.

George Corwin was the Sheriff of Essex County, Massachusetts in 1692, and I was the Sheriff of Essex County almost 300 years later. As horrible and brutal as his treatment of accused witches was, I wonder if we have improved ourselves that dramatically over the last three centuries, or are we as cruel now in our punishments as Corwin was then? Possibly we're just more subtle in our cruelty. Was the electric chair, introduced in America in 1890, leading over 4,300 people to their death, and half as many awaiting a similar fate, more humane than hanging or beheading? Is chemical castration, which is now being considered nation-wide as a punishment , any less brutal than having to watch your bowels being burned under your nose? Is the public aware, I wonder, that over one million American men are raped in prison per year, as compared to 200,000 women on the streets? Is lethal injection the punishment of choice for a wise and enlightened society? I ask you these questions, for being an old law enforcement man, I certainly can't comment.– all law enforcement types are for capital punishment, aren't they? *Lock 'em up and throw away the key.* Isn't that our pat response for the treatment of criminals? The pendulum is swinging back, it seems, and for answers to our growing crime problems we seem to be falling back into the burning, boiling and beheading mindset of our forefathers. Hopefully we will not regress, but will seek new means and methods to solve our criminal problems, keeping in mind that cruelty is no deterrent, nor was it ever a solution.

Nix's Mate, once a thirteen acre island in Boston Harbor, was where pirates were sometimes hanged and buried, and often gibbeted. However, when an innocent sailor was hanged here for piracy, the island sank, and only a rock wall and pyramid mark the site today. Old engraving of Nix's Mate from the "Atlantic Neptune," 1781.

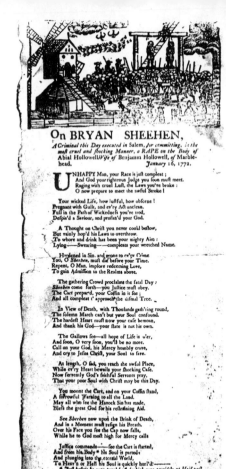

On BRYAN SHEEHAN,

A Criminal this Day executed in Salem, for committing, in the most cruel and shocking Manner, a RAPE on the Body of Abial Hollowell, Wife of Benjamin Hollowell, of Marblehead.

January 16, 1772.

UNHAPPY Man, your Race is juſt compleat ;
  And God your righteous Judge you ſoon muſt meet.
  Raging with cruel Luſt, the Laws you're broke :
  O now prepare to meet the awful Stroke !

Your wicked Life, how luſtful, how obſcene !
Pregnant with Guilt, and ev'ry Act unclean.
Full in the Path of Wickedneſs you're trod,
Deſpiſ'd a Saviour, and profan'd your God.

A Thought on Chriſt you never could beſtow,
But vainly hop'd his Laws to overthrow.
To whore and drink has been your mighty Aim :
Lying——Swearing——compleats your wretched Name.

Hardened in Sin, and prone to ev'ry Crime
You, O Sheehan, muſt die before your Time.
Repent, O Man, implore redeeming Love,
To gain Admiſſion to the Realms above.

The gathering Crowd proclaims the fatal Day :
Sheehan come forth—you Juſtice muſt obey.
The Cart prepar'd, your Coffin in it ſee ;
And all compleat t' approach the diſmal Tree.

In View of Death, with Thouſands gath'ring round,
The ſolemn March can't but your Soul confound.
The hardeſt Heart can't now your caſe bemoan,
And thank his God—your ſtate is not his own.

The Gallows ſee—all hope of Life is o'er,
And ſoon, O very ſoon, you'll be no more.
Call on your God, his Mercy humbly crave,
And cry to Jeſus Chriſt, your Soul to ſave.

At length, O ſad, you reach the awful Place,
While ev'ry Heart bewails your ſhocking Caſe.
Now fervently God's faithful Servants pray,
That your poor Soul with Chriſt may be this Day.

You mount the Cart, and on your Coffin ſtand,
A ſorrowful Warning to all the Land.
May all who ſee the Havock Sin has made,
Bleſs the great God for his reſtraining Aid.

See Sheehan now upon the Brink of Death,
And in a Moment muſt reſign his Breath.
Over his Face you ſee the Cap now falls,
While he to God moſt high for Mercy calls

Juſtice commands——ſee the Cart is ſtarted,
And from his Body the his Soul is parted—
And plunging into the eternal World,
To Heav'n or Hell his Soul is quickly hurl'd:——
  Juſt before he was turn'd off, (which was preciſely at Half paſt Three o'Clock,) *he deſired his Body might be given to Dr. Kaſt of Salem for diſſection.*

Printed and Sold oppoſite the Priſon in Queen-ſtreet, at which Place, may be had his Life and Character.

The original broadbill sold in great quantities to some 12,000 people who came to see Bryan Sheehan hang at "Execution Hill," Winter Island, Salem (shown below). He was hanged in January of 1772, the first to be executed in Essex County since the witch hysteria of 1692. The sketch is of Stephen Clark who was hanged in the same spot as Sheehan in 1822. His crime was arson at Newburyport when he was 15 years old. The authorities waited until he was 17 to hang him.
Broadbill courtesy of the Essex Institute, Salem, MA.

Bibliography

Acts and Resolves, Public and Private of the Province of Massachusetts, Boston, MA (21 volumes) – 1896-1922.

Austin, Jane, Nantucket Scraps, James R. Osgood Co., Boston, MA – 1883.

Bleackley, Horace, The Hangmen of England, Chapman and Hall, London, England.

Boorstin, Daniel J., The Americans: The Colonial Experience, Random House, New York – 1958.

Brooks, Henry M., Strange and Curious Punishments, Ticknor and Company, Boston, MA – 1887.

Browning, Frank and Gerassi, John, The American Way of Crime, G.P. Putnam's Sons, New York – 1980.

Chandler, Peleg, W., American Criminal Trials, Little Brown, Boston – 1841.

Drake, Samuel Adams, Nooks and Corners of the New England Coast, Harper and Brothers Publishers, New York – 1875.

Earle, Alice Morse, Curious Punishments of Bygone Days, Herbert S. Stone and Company, Chicago, IL – 1896.

Furnas, J.C., The Americans – A Social History of the U.S., 1587-1914, G.P. Putnam's Sons, New York – 1969.

Greene, Lorenzo, J., The Negro in Colonial New England – 1620-1776, New York – 1942.

Hofstadter, Richard, America at 1750: A Social Portrait, Alfred A. Knopf, New York – 1971.

Holbrook, Stewart H., Great True Stories of Crime, Mystery and Detection, The Reader's Digest Association, Pleasantville, NY – 1965.

Horwood, Harold and Butts, Ed, Bandits and Privateers, Goodread Biographies, Halifax, Nova Scotia – 1951.

Kraus, Michael, The United States to 1865, The University of Michigan Press, Ann Arbor, MI – 1969.

Lawrence, Henry W., The Not-Quite Puritans, Little, Brown and Co., Boston, MA – 1928.

Lawrence, Robert Means, New England Colonial Life, The Cosmos Press, Inc., Cambridge, MA 1927.

Makris, John N. (edited by), Boston Murders, Duell, Sloan and Pearce, Inc. New York, NY – 1948.

Marsella, Paul D., Crime and Community in Early Massachusetts, Essex County, Ginn Custom Publishing, Lexington, MA – 1983.

Mather, Cotton, Pillars of Salt, B. Green and J. Allen, Boston – 1699.

Morgan, Edmund S., The Puritans and Sex, New England Quarterly XV, Boston, MA – December, 1942.

Parks, Roger (edited by), The New England Galaxy, Globe Pequot Press, Chester, CT – 1980.

Piersen, William D., Black Yankees, The University of Massachusetts Press, Amherst, MA – 1988.

Potter, John Deane, The Art of Hanging, A.S. Barnes and Company, Inc., Cranbury, New Jersey – 1965.

Savage, Edward H., Recollectioms of a Boston Police Officer, Patterson-Smith, Montcain, New Jersey – 1971.

Smith, Abbott E., Colonists in Bondage: White Servitude and Convict-Labor in America, W.W. Norton Company, New York – 1971.

Stiles, Henry Reed, Bundling, A George Dawson Book, Applewood Books, Chester, CT – 1872.

Van Doren, Mark (edited by), Samuel Sewall's Diary, Macy-Masivs Publishers – 1927.

Willison, George F., Saints and Strangers, Reynal and Hitchcock, New York – 1945.